NATIVE AMERICANS

INTERDISCIPLANARY PERSPECTIVES

edited by
JOHN R. WUNDER
CYNTHIA WILLIS ESQUEDA
UNIVERSITY OF NEBRASKA-LINCOLN

A ROUTLEDGE SERIES

Political Principles & Indian Sovereignty

Thurman Lee Hester, Jr.

LONDON AND NEW YORK

Published 2001 by Routledge
711 Third Avenue, New York, NY 10017, USA
2 Park Square, Milton Park, Abingdon, Oxfordshire OX14 4RN

First issued in paperback 2016

Routledge is an imprint of the Taylor & Francis Group, an informa business

Copyright © 2001 by Thurman Lee Hester, Jr.

All rights reserved. No part of this book may be reprinted or reproduced or utilized in any form or by any electronic, mechanical, or other means, now known or hereafter invented, including photocopying and recording, or in any information storage or retrieval system, without written permission from the publishers.

Library of Congress Cataloging-in-Publication Data is available from the Library of Congress.

Publisher's Note
The publisher has gone to great lengths to ensure the quality of this reprint but points out that some imperfections in the original may be apparent.

ISBN 13: 978-1-138-97884-3 (pbk)
ISBN 13: 978-0-8153-4023-2 (hbk)

Contents

Foreword	vii
Introduction	1
1. Current Problems	5
2. Settler Imperialism	19
3. Removal	31
4. Decimation and War	53
5. Allotment to the Present	67
6. A Case for Sovereignty	91
Appendix A: The Bureau of Indian Affairs Mission Statement	*117*
Appendix B: Mission Statement of The Office of Indian Education Programs	*118*
Appendix C: Mission Statement of the Indian Health Service	*119*
Appendix D: Treaty Excerpts	*120*
Works Cited	*131*
Cases Cited	*137*
Index	*139*

Foreword
Chief Gregory Pyle of the Choctaw Nation of Oklahoma

During the past 400 years, many groups have tried to control the Indian people. The United States Government has been regulating us for most of the past 200 years. During these centuries, at places like Wheelock Academy, we were told we shouldn't be speaking our Native language, and that we should give up our culture. The Federal Government sent Indians all over the country under the Relocation Act. After generations of Federal control, in 1971, the Five Tribes were finally allowed to elect their own leaders again.

Since that time, the Choctaw Nation of Oklahoma has been evolving and progressing. Though we've had a constitutional form of government for about 100 years, we've reformed our constitution to meet new challenges. As of April, 2000, the tribe handles about $225 million a year. 70% of this tremendous budget is from our businesses, and only about 30% is from federal grants. We are moving away from the forced dependency of the past more and more every day.

It is wonderful to see people striving to continue our heritage and language. The Choctaw Nation of Oklahoma has put tribal monies into a teaching program so that everyone who is interested in learning the Choctaw language will have an opportunity to do so. In addition to classes on a face-to-face basis, the tribe has sponsored satellite classes and are also offering classes on the internet. Opporutnities like the Language Program all started 29 years ago when the tribes were once more allowed to elect their own leaders and run their own government.

Tribal sovereignty is the life blood of American Indians' ability to maintain our culture, heritage, and right of self-determination. For many years, our people were on the bottom rung of the social and economic ladder in the country. After the passage of PL 93-638, Indian Self-Determination Act, the U.S. policy changed to one of tribal self-determination and economic development. American Indian tribes were encouraged to become self-sufficient, free of federal financial dependency. Needless to say, Indian tribes welcomed this new policy and embraced it with great enthusiasm. Every dollar Indian Tribes make and put back into assistance for our citizens is a dollar less we are dependent on the Federal or State Government. If tribes were not considered sovereign entities and not recipients of federal funding, the burden of responsibility of care for these citizens would fall back on the Federal or State Government.

We have worked hard to find ways to generate revenues to finance this goal of financial independence. Unlike local, state and federal governments, Indian tribes have little or no tax base or ways to raise revenues as other conventional governments have.

We began to look at commercial endeavors, such as hotels, resorts, truck stops, manufacturing, and real estate rental properties such as shopping centers. Sovereignty has been central to these efforts. Unfortunately, sovereignty and particularly sovereign immunity are among the most divisive issues that face Congress each year. Opinions on this issue run very strong on both sides.

The sovereignty of tribal nations can be a positive force for all parties—Indian and non-Indian alike — when utilized appropriately. The Choctaw Nation conducts business with our non-Indian business partners and with the State of Oklahoma while preserving our sovereign immunity. For many years we could not agree with our state government in Oklahoma about state taxation practices. It was a very difficult situation, both sides were adamant. But in the end, we were able to put aside these differences and arrive at agreements which work to everyone's benefit. And we did it without sacrificing our immunity. In fact, I submit that without this sovereignty, we may have never been able to reach compacts with the state in fuel and tobacco taxation.

These compacts were not easy. There were endless disputes, roadblocks, and land mines which could have blown up in our faces. Negotiations were tough and sometimes downright contentious. But in the end, our determination on both sides to come to an agreement and put these issues behind us prevailed. Both of our governments could then return to our most important duty of providing for the general welfare of our citizens.

We must provide jobs, promote education and care for those of our citizens who cannot care for themselves. These and other serious tribal obligations illustrate why Indian tribes engaging in commercial activities are not like private corporations or other businesses. We engage in business activities to provide revenues to operate our governments. Our profits are not used to make individuals wealthy or to compensate shareholders. We use our profits for such basic things as educating our children, improving our people's healthcare, providing safe and decent housing and other causes – things which most Americans take for granted. These are the goals and purposes of Choctaw tribal enterprises and tribal governments throughout the United States.

Because of our gaming revenues, economic development ventures and money earned from our Fuel Tax Compact with the State of Oklahoma, the Choctaw Nation of Oklahoma has begun tribally funded programs to provide eyeglasses, dentures, hearing aids and other medical equipment needs to our tribal members. We have been able to provide funds for Boys & Girls Clubs in several counties and able to partner with local public schools in providing after-school recreation programs for youth in socially disadvantaged areas.

This is of utmost importance in a state with one of the highest teen pregnancy rates in the nation. By providing structured, supervised activities for young people in the afternoons and on weekends we will have one of the greatest drug prevention programs possible. These program are wonderful examples of how tribal sovereignty benefits both the American Indian and non-Indian communities. By sharing state, federal, private and tribal resources, we constructed an American Indian Center at Eastern Oklahoma State College in Latimer County, which will reduce the dropout rate by providing counseling and academic tutorial assistance for our Indian students. The Choctaw Nation contributed $1.2 million of tribal funds to this project.

The Choctaw Nation built a new hospital, not by waiting for the federal government to build it for us but by utilizing existing IHS dollars, fuel tax dollars, gaming dollars and tribal economic development dollars. By the Choctaw Nation partnering with agencies such as Little Dixie Community Action Agency and by utilizing the services of both, we are able to provide more job opportunities for everyone in the community. Please understand, my priority is the Choctaw people, but I want to stress that when we succeed in business, everyone benefits. Our businesses provide jobs, additional income for the area, additional tax dollars for the community and allow opportunities for retail sales. Gaming and travel plazas have been successful ventures for the Choctaw Nation. These ventures have provided a tremendous means to support additional businesses, social programs, education programs and health programs of the Choctaw Nation. I would like to point out that tribal business revenues allow between 1,300 and 1,500 higher education scholarships to be awarded to Choctaw youth. This is self-determination at it's best.Since we were "discovered" about 500 years ago, there have been many attempts to do away with Indian tribes. The Self-Determination Act of the 1970's marked a turning point for the tribes to regain their governments. The re-recognition of the Indian sovereignty under Self-Determination and later acts is not only beneficial to all involved, but it is simple justice as this book shows.

Introduction

> *One of the finest things about being an Indian is that everyone is interested in your "plight." Other groups have difficulties, predicaments, quandaries, problems, or troubles. Traditionally we Indians have had a "plight."*
>
> —*Vine Deloria, Jr.*[1]

This book is a philosophical examination of the Indian "plight." It will examine some of the problems facing Native American people and their nations here in the United States and it will argue for a solution to those problems. The solution sought will be to implement true sovereignty for Native American nations. Though the rhetoric of U.S. law asserts that Indian nations have "inherent" and "retained" sovereignty it will be argued that the form this "sovereignty" has taken make it at best a form of self-governance and at worst a cruel joke.

Modern philosophical arguments that might support Indian sovereignty will be avoided. Such theoretical arguments are unlikely to have any real effect. They would involve complex problems of group rights and social obligations, problematic notions in themselves and unlikely to affect the policymakers in Washington D.C.. Indeed, as Nicholas Rescher pointed out,

> Do American philosophers exert influence? Here the critical question is: Upon whom? Certainly as far as the wider society is concerned it must be said that the answer is emphatically nega-

tive. American philosophers are not opinion-shapers: they do not have access to the media, to the political establishment, to the 'think tanks' that seek to mold public opinion. In so far as they exert an external influence at all, it is confined to the *academics* of other fields.[2]

Rescher believes that one of the causes of this inefficacy is the inaccessibility of modern U.S. philosophy. Overspecialization has made it overly technical. This book will attempt to be accessible and thus more effective. Ongoing injustices that have endured for hundreds of years should end. Since the group to be persuaded is the Federal Government of the United States, this work must proceed from premises accepted by that government. Thus rather than utilizing theoretical frameworks common to modern academic American philosophy, it will attempt to use the stated philosophy of the U.S. Government as revealed in laws, official documents and public pronouncements by competent officials. This doesn't mean theory will be completely eschewed. However, it does recognize that a new theory is unlikely to have any significant practical consequences in the short term.

Besides this methodological commitment to practical effects through applied philosophical reason, the author believes that few new theories are really necessary to deal with most of the current problems. The laws that have limited, on this view ended, the sovereignty of Native nations are fundamentally inconsistent with the supposed guiding principles and laws of the United States. This paper will show that many of the problems faced by Native nations were caused or worsened by laws, policies and court decisions that are inconsistent with these principles. If this position can be maintained then it would seem that the problems should be amenable to existing laws and theories.

In form, this work will constitute a cumulative argument consisting of a series of individual arguments against existing Federal Indian law. Together they will form a tapestry supporting Indian sovereignty. Many of the arguments will be interconnected and fairly complex, due to the complexities of Indian law. But in the end, the reader should come to realize that the basic issues are relatively simple despite the complexities of the law. Indeed, it will turn out that the complexities have arisen precisely because the principles are simple.

The first chapter will provide a *prima facie* case for change, showing some of the problems faced by Native American nations.

In addition, it will examine the causes of these problems. This will allow for a link to be made between the problems and U.S. policy. Chapters Two through Five will provide an overview of U.S. policy, uninterrupted by extended argumentation. This narrative will help to make clear the contradictory nature of U.S. law and policy by its rapid juxtaposition of the varying laws through time. This policy history will also provide the final link between the ills suffered by Native American people today and the laws and policies of the United States. Chapter Six will draw on evidence from the preceding Chapters, arguing that since decreased sovereignty led to the problems, we can hope that increased sovereignty will decrease the problems. It will then show that the historical denial of Indian sovereignty was and is inconsistent with the fundamental guiding principles of the United States, while the current assertion of Indian sovereignty in Federal law is no less problematic. In doing so, it will also suggest how this fundamental inconsistency has created the complex structure of Indian law. Finally, a few recommendations will be made concerning the policy of Indian Nations toward the United States as well as what U.S. policy should be toward Native Nations.

Notes

1. Vine Deloria, Jr., *Custer Died for Your Sins*, (Norman and London: University of Oklahoma Press, 1988), 1.
2. Nicholas Rescher, "American Philosophy," *The Oxford Companion to Philosophy*, Ted Honderich, ed. (New York: Oxford University Press, 1995), 27.

CHAPTER ONE
Current Problems

> *If you multiply every social problem in America by 10—high school dropouts, suicide among teenagers, alcohol and drug abuse, death by violence, disease—you have what Indians go through.*
> —Senator Ben Nighthorse Campbell[1]

Many complex problems face Native Americans and their tribes. The problems can be divided into a few broad categories including economics, education and health care. Obviously these categories are not exhaustive, nor are the problems in any of them isolate. The problems can and do interact. Despite this complexity, we can lay many of the problems *qua* problems out fairly simply. We'll allow some of the complexities to creep in when examining causes. To the extent that the U.S. Government assumes responsibility for Indian welfare, problems in these areas may indicate problems in U.S. policy. Whether U.S. policy can be shown to be the cause, if the U.S. assumes this responsibility in these areas then the problems enumerated here certainly provide a *prima facie* case for critical policy review.

Income, one of the standards of welfare accepted by the U.S. Government, shows a significant difference between groups and particularly between Native Americans and Whites despite the fact the Federal Government has a goal of improving the economic opportunities of Native Americans.[2] American Indians had a median family income of $21,619 in 1990, the most recent year reported.[3]

The median family income for Whites that year was $41,922.[4] The Indian figures are averaged out over all the tribes, but for some tribes the picture is even worse. Among the Navajo, median family income was only $13,940.[5] The Cherokee, Choctaw and perhaps the Iroquois[6] help to offset the lower figures of the Navajo and others.

The figures appear even starker when poverty levels are considered. The percentage of White families below the poverty line is 9.47, while some 27.2 percent of Indian families[8] live below the poverty line. As with the income figures, there is significant variation between tribes. The Navajo again appear to come out worst with some 47.3 percent[9] of families below the poverty line. Even among the best off tribes you are roughly twice as likely as a White to be poverty-stricken.[10]

Another problem area is education. The Federal Government of the United States has accepted significant responsibility for Indian education through a variety of programs including the Johnson-O'Malley Act as well as more general responsibility through the Bureau of Indian Affairs.[11] Despite the importance attached to Native American education, only 65 percent of American Indians have a high school diploma and only 9.4 percent have a bachelor's degree.[12] Among the White population 83.1 percent have graduated high school, while some 22.9 percent have a college degree.[13]

Unfortunately this disparity in Indian education is unlikely to change soon. For it to change in the short term there would have to be a significant increase in current graduation rates. Even over the long haul, there would have to be equivalent graduation rates for Indians as a group to achieve educational parity with their White counterparts. The graduation rate is not higher, nor on par, but is actually lower. Native Americans are roughly 8/10ths of one percent of the population. Assuming even distribution among the other segments of the population,[14] about 8/10ths of one percent of all graduating classes at all levels should be composed of Native Americans. This is not the case. In higher education, Native Americans made up only 5/10ths of one percent of all those graduating with a bachelor's degree; 4/10ths of one percent of all those receiving master's degrees; and 3/10ths of one percent of all those receiving doctoral degrees.[15] These figures show that the disparity in education level will continue for some time and will even worsen if current trends aren't reversed.

Though poverty and education are certainly problems for Indian people, the most obvious problems are in health care. Despite the fact that the U.S. Government has taken responsibility for Indian health care through the Indian Health Service,[16] there are enormous disparities between Native Americans and other segments of U.S. society. American Indians are 1.1 times as likely to die before reaching their first birthday, 1.6 times more likely to die between one and four years of age, 1.4 times as likely to die between five and fourteen, and twice as likely to die between fifteen and twenty-four when compared to the rest of the U.S. population.[17] The ratio of American Indian death rates to those of the overall population for other age groups continue at these elevated levels until age sixty-five. The statistics are even worse when compared only to the White population. From age twenty-five to age forty-four, American Indians are more than twice as likely to die as Whites. Every year from age five to age fifty-four Indians are at least 1.5 time as likely to die as whites. About the only good news is that Native Americans who manage to reach seventy-four can expect to live somewhat longer on average than the rest of the population. Death rates from that age on are somewhat lower than either that of whites or that of all races.[18]

Given that the U.S. Government has, as some of its goals, the economic well being of Indians; the education of Indian people; and the health of its Native American citizens; it would appear that it has failed. This argues weakly for a discontinuation of past U.S. policy. A more forceful case would require a clearer link between U.S. policy and its failure to meet these goals. In each instance we must examine the causes for failure and then see if these are attributable to the policies. Even if the policies are at fault, it may be that the causes are not tied sovereignty *per se*. So, if we are going to call for 'true' sovereignty, then the link must be directly to elements of U.S. policy that have ended the sovereignty of Native American. The remainder of this chapter begins this process by laying out the causes of these problems.

What causes poverty? Many theories have been advanced to account for poverty, especially in countries like the U.S. where abundance is taken to be the norm. Without any significant theorizing, we can certainly say that wholesale dispossession of wealth and sources of wealth would be a cause. If U.S. Government policies have caused such dispossession, then these policies should be changed.

Besides obvious causes like dispossession, there are numerous other causes that may have a bearing on the current state of Native finance. Unfortunately, decades of research on poverty have not yielded a comprehensive theory as to its causes. As Syed Samad wrote, "The basic configuration of poverty and its global distribution are fairly well known and documented. Its causes and consequences, however, continue to generate heated debates, leading occasionally to polarized positions."[19] Even worse, he maintains that poverty research in the United States has been, ". . . anchored in the ideological leanings of the researcher-analyst."[20] Though highly politicized and without a single comprehensive theory, or even a leading theory, poverty researchers still have a lot to offer in the way of possible causes.

Theories on the causes of poverty have historically been divided into the following families:[21] Locality and demography; economic structures and policies; social structural explanations; culture and individual behaviors; poverty policies as causative agencies; and power and poverty. Within each of the families there are a number of specific theories, though the causes presented within each family are fairly homogeneous.

Locality and other demographic theories often cite the differences between urban and rural populations. Rural populations are usually poorer than urban populations, though the large number of urban poor in the U.S. requires explaining as well.[22] Poverty of rural populations may be caused by a variety of factors including the relatively low value placed on agricultural and raw material production labor.[23] An intriguing view concerning the urban/rural dichotomy is that there is a persistent bias toward urban development, caused by a wide variety of factors including the centralization of governmental power in urban areas and the fact that most governmental officials not only live in these urban seats of power but are originally drawn from them.[24] Since most Indian people live in rural areas, this bias may be a factor in their poverty.

While this explanation may provide insight into rural Indian poverty, there would have to be some other explanation for the poverty of urban Indians within this paradigm. There are a variety of locality explanations concerning the urban poor, but we need not examine most of them since they are concerned with urban immigrants from foreign nations or with minority groups that have lived in urban areas for some time. Native American are relative newcomers to U.S. cities, a large number of them having come to the city within only the last generation or two. As such their poverty is a kind of "hold over" of their rural poverty, the well recognized "vicious cycle."[25] On this view poverty is self-perpetuating because of the relative inequality of poor people's starting point in our society. Overcoming poverty takes time, if it can be overcome at all. Locality theorists accept the vicious cycle explanation for urban poor in circumstances like those of most urban Indians.

Economic structure and policy theorists are the most prolific in their range of explanations. Since they are looking at particular structures and policies, their theories vary from country to country and from year to year. In addition they may be discussing the effects of specific legislation on particular groups. Thus much of this theorizing is not going to be relevant in our search for the causes of Native American poverty. Only one of the major families of policy theories may fit Native Americans: Those used for colonized people. These explanations say that the poverty is part of the legacy of colonialism. "Colonial rule deliberately enforced industrial backwardness for reasons of commercial interest, destroyed self-confidence, created habits of dependency."[26] Even on short reflection, we can imagine many ways in which colonial rule would affect a group's later development. Clearly, much wealth could be siphoned off during the colonial period as the colonizers took advantage of the raw materials in the colony. To the extent that we see the U.S. as colonizers in North America, successors to the colonial powers they supplanted, this model may help to explain Indian poverty.

According to social structural theories,

> The socially vulnerable become the economically vulnerable. They suffer discrimination in the labor market because of prejudice and stereotyping. Marginalized people, whether they are demarcated as women, minority groups, or recent immigrants, may have difficulty in getting jobs (indeed, may be barred by law or custom from seeking paid work or working in certain protected activities) and may receive low wages when they are employed.[27]

To the extent that Native Americans are marginalized people, this too may be a part of the puzzle.

Cultural explanations are among the most favored today. The assumption is that the poor themselves do something that makes them poor, or keeps them poor. Though some theorists stress individual behaviors, most emphasize the "culture of poverty"[28] as the origin of these individual behaviors. People are acculturated into poverty, learning behaviors that go with their status. Unfortunately, most of these behaviors extend poverty. Few are of any aid in trying to escape it.

In trying to understand the psychology of individuals within the culture of poverty, Theodore Sarbin[29] identified three important factors: The conceptualization of time; linguistic codes; and locus of control. Poor people's concept of time is more oriented in the present, not allowing them to defer gratification in order to achieve longer term success.[30] Their linguistic codes are simplified and aimed at reinforcing and implementing the social structure rather than conveying information.[31] In addition, those in the culture of poverty believe that external forces over which they have no power ultimately control their destiny.[32] With external forces in control, they would clearly believe any move to escape poverty was futile. This latter seems likely to be applicable to Native Americans as we later examine U.S. policies.

Poverty policies themselves have been viewed as potential causes of the very blights they seek to eradicate. If such policies provide incentives for the poor not to seek work, then they are liable to perpetuate poverty. Those who lived through the "Reagan era" well-know the pervasiveness of this view, which is still a major factor in current policymaking. Though these views probably have some applicability to Native Americans, at least one critic has suggested that even typical liberal views when applied to the problems of the world's indigenous people, leads them to the wrong conclusions.

> It all adds up to culture-busting, often without much interest in the problems, except to cheer when it happens fast. It also adds up to a kind of cultural arrogance on the part of the West which makes one pause. I'm right — you're wrong. Maybe — but that isn't exactly what the old-fashioned liberals had in mind. But, as we said before, what else have we got.
>
> If you buy the necessity of busting up cultures, there is another problem. How do you bust them up efficiently? We don't want American Indian type results.[33]

Power and poverty theories place the blame for poverty at the feet of those who wield power, the privileged groups that seem to exist in most societies. It is not surprising that, already having power, they would have not only the motive but the means to keep it.

At this point it should also be obvious just how intertwined these theories are. Power theories posit inequality of power as a source of poverty, but so too did the rural/urban theorists as well as the legacy of colonialism camp. The poor are an out-group either because they were rural, of the wrong race or ethnicity. Of course in most cases they were "all of the above." It is not surprising when social structures favor the rich and poverty programs fail to alleviate the burdens of the poor. Poverty begins to look more like a "family resemblance" in which a large number of characteristics are common to the family and the poorest tend to have most of the characteristics. Unfortunately, Native Americans seem to be among those that have most of the characteristics for poverty.

Given their poverty, it is perhaps not surprising that they should also be poorly educated. But besides poverty are there other reasons why Indian education lags behind that of other segments of society? To the extent that education is available to Indian people,[34] why do they not avail themselves of the opportunity? Perhaps it is because they lack motivation.

> The key to effective educational experience lies in motivation. The child will exert himself with whatever capacity he can muster when he is working toward goals that are real and meaningful in terms of motives and purposes, on the one hand, and his background of ability and experience on the other. His need for self-enhancement will not permit him to do otherwise.... On the contrary, to the extent that the child is forced to participate in experiences that are not related to the attainment of his goals and purposes, aversive effects—apathy, superficial learning, frustration, negative attitudes, misbehavior, maladjustment—are likely to follow.[35]

This seems all the more likely when we realize that other factors, such as intelligence have a fairly low correlation with educational success, about .50 and that motivation is generally take to account for this difference.[36] A fairly standard account of motivation holds that motivation is a factor of two main forces: the individual's expectation of reaching a goal and the importance of the goal to the person.[37] That these standard factors taken from well-known education texts are applicable to Indian students is well-recognized. As stated in *Teaching American Indian Students,*

> The fundamental consensus that Indian children are like most other children provides a foundation for one of the book's major assumptions: teaching Indian children is no different than teach-

ing other children. This does not mean that Indian children are the same as non-Indian children. . . . Neither appreciation nor respect are possible without knowing the children's cultural and environmental backgrounds.[38]

So, it would appear that educational success is more likely among those Indian children that are motivated to learn methods that will enable them to achieve their own goals and purposes. We would thus expect that policies which hampered the achievement of goals or which made the goals appear unattainable, would militate against the successful education of Native American children.

In the area of health care, the real key is why Native Americans experience such high death rates when compared to other Americans. Age-adjusted mortality rates comparing Native Americans and all U.S. races show that American Indians have a 440 percent greater chance of dying of tuberculosis, 430 percent greater chance of dying of alcoholism, 165 percent greater chance of dying by accident, 154 percent greater chance of dying from diabetes mellitus, 50 percent greater chance of being killed, 46 percent greater chance of dying from pneumonia or influenza and a 43 percent greater chance of committing suicide.[39] Unfortunately, even this mass of statistics isn't quite sufficient to truly define the problem. For example, though tuberculosis is far more prevalent among Native Americans than among the general populace, it isn't one of the major causes of death for any age group. Though the rate of tuberculosis mortality is shocking when compared the rest of the U.S. population, the actual number of deaths is fairly small.

The real culprits[40] behind the startling death rates are accidents (the number one cause of death between ages one and forty-four), suicide (the second leading cause of death between ages fifteen and twenty-four and fourth leading cause from twenty-five to forty-four), homicide (third leading cause of death between ages one and forty-four) and chronic liver disease/cirrhosis (second leading cause of death between ages twenty-five and forty-four). In general the ranking of these causes is the same for the U.S. population as a whole, though the rates are greatly exaggerated for American Indians. The real anomalies are suicide and chronic liver disease/cirrhosis. These causes were actually ranked higher among Native Americans in various age groups than among the populace as a whole. When one considers that the main cause of chronic liver disease/cirrhosis is alcohol abuse; that many accidental deaths are alcohol related (e.g. drunk driving fatalities); and that alcohol often plays a role in suicide and homicide, a trend begins to appear. Unfortunately this trend is one which many would like to ignore. It has led to the common stereotype of the "drunken Indian,"[41] a stereotype that is not only unjust but has led to bad scholarship and bizarre policy recommendations.

Probably the most famous example of bad scholarship in the area of Indian alcohol use is the study[42] which suggests, wrongly, that Indians metabolize alcohol more slowly than other racial groups. Unfortunately, in exposing the shortcomings of this study and exploding other myths concerning Indian alcohol use, some researchers have gone a bit too far. Phillip May[43] explodes the myth that alcoholism is the number one health problem among American Indians by equivocating between *alcoholism* and *alcohol abuse*. As he says, "More accurately, alcohol abuse and alcoholism combine to be the leading cause of mortality." This is certainly comforting.

Recommended solutions to the high alcohol related mortality rate sometimes suffer from the desire to avoid stereotyping Indians as problem drinkers. One study[44] suggests that alcohol related accidental deaths like those involving car crashes or pedestrian hypothermia can be reduced by bringing the alcohol to the Indians—eliminating prohibition on those reservations that still have it. Barring that, they suggest carpools for patrons and reflector stripes for pedestrians might help. The closest that the study comes to suggesting a decrease in consumption is a recommendation to limit the hours of operation of bars near reservations. Prevention, treatment and rehabilitation are mentioned only in passing and only in the final sentence. Though it is impossible to prove that the desire to avoid stereotyping was behind the choice to linger on solutions to the final as opposed to the proximal causes of death, it certainly seems likely. The fact that the same volume of the *Journal of the American Medical Association* that carried this study also carried an article[45] against stereotyping Indians as drunks is suggestive.

Avoiding stereotypes doesn't make the problem go away. Alcohol is arguably the number one killer of Native Americans. Dropping prohibition or busing Indians to bars is merely treating a symptom. It might help to alleviate some of the accidental deaths but only at the risk of increasing the longer term health problems like cirrhosis. To truly end the problem, the drinking should be curbed.

In the search for causes, we are aided by those that have exploded the myths. It is clear that there is no cause for drinking that is unique to Native Americans. Indians drink for the same reasons that other people do.[46] Swinson and Eaves[47] summarily state that, "People who have high personal motivation toward drug-taking tend to originate from groups which commonly produce inadequate, insecure, tense members, who are subject to little in the way of effective controls against deviant behavior." Though rather disingenuously put, this statement must be taken seriously. Forrest[48] provides other reasons saying, "Identity and role confusion are precursors to alcoholism and alcohol abuse."

In quantitative studies, many different instruments have been used to test various psychological factors. Among these is "Locus of Control" (LOC). Though early studies of LOC using the Rotter scale had conflicting results, newer studies using the Levenson scale have shown a correlation between alcoholism and external LOC[49] as well as a correlation between a shift to internal LOC and treatment success.[50] This is extremely significant, since we have also seen a link between external LOC and poverty in the work of Theodore Sarbin during our examination of the causes of poverty. A study comparing LOC of Indians and non-Indians in Oklahoma showed that Native Americans generally had a much higher external LOC than Whites.[51] This study showed a LOC "Powerful Other" of 24.13 for Indians as compared to 20.46 for Caucasians and an LOC "Chance" of 26.71 versus 20.92. Clearly Native Americans tend to feel that they do not control their own lives.

Many of the problems facing Native Americans seem to be related to an external locus of control. Poverty and alcoholism are related directly, with standardized studies of LOC showing a strong correlation. In addition, the commonsensical nature of such explanation as well as the power of the explanation is obvious. People who believe they have little or no control over their own lives might despair of escaping their fate, take no positive action, and could well end up seeking solace in drugs or alcohol. Even standard education theories cite motivation, in particular the efficacy of the education in meeting the goals of the student. If the student's destiny is controlled by outside forces, or if the student believes it is so, then why bother?

In our examination of U.S. policy, we should be on the lookout for laws and policies that take control of Indian life out of their hands; or which would lead them to believe that control had been wrested. Directly harmful policies should also be examined not only for their harm, but as further reason for an external locus of control among Native Americans. Other policies that would be in line with the causes outlined previously, such as dispossession, should also be noted.

Notes

1. Quoted by Rochelle Stanfield, "Getting Out the Tribal Vote," *National Journal,* (Washington D.C.: National Journal Inc., 1992), v 24, n 30, p 1756.
2. See Appendix A for the mission statement of the Bureau of Indian Affairs, which specifically cites this as a goal.
3. U.S. Bureau of the Census, *Statistical Abstract of the United States 1995,* (Washington, D.C.: U.S. Government Printing Office), Table 52.
4. Ibid., table 49.
5. Ibid., table 52.
6. Median family incomes for all of these tribes were well above the median across all tribes, however, none of them was as much as 2/3 the median income of Whites. The highest by far, the Iroquois, may actually have been misreported as noted by the Census Bureau. Ibid.
7. Ibid., table 49.
8. Ibid., table 52.
9. Ibid.
10. Mathematical comparison of tables 49 and 52 Ibid.
11. See Appendix B for the mission statement of the Office of Indian Education Programs, showing the importance the U.S. Government attaches to Indian education.
12. Ibid,. table 52.
13. Ibid., table 49 and mathematical interpretation of data.
14. A bad assumption, but one that should, if anything make the comparative graduation rates appear higher than they are.
15. Ibid., table 303.
16. See mission statement of the Indian Health Service in Appendix C, showing the importance that the U.S. Government attaches to Indian health..
17. Statistics in this paragraph are taken from, U.S. Indian Health Service, *Trends In Indian Health—1994,* (Washington D.C.: Department of Health and Human Services, 1994), Table 4.10, p 55.
18. Ibid., 55.
19. Syed Abdus Samad, "The Present Situation in Poverty Research," in *Poverty: A Global Review* eds. Else Oyen, S. M. Miller and Syed Abdus

Samad, (Oslo and Paris: Scandinavian University Press and UNESCO, 1996), 33.

20. Ibid, 43.

21. The general taxonomy presented here is taken from S. M. Miller, "The Great Chain of Poverty Explanations," ibid, 569–586 and informed by George Thomas, *Poverty in the Non-Metropolitan South: A Causal Explanation*, (Lexington Massachusetts: Lexington Books, 1972), chap. 3, which suggested the idea of applying a variety of theories in analyzing specific instances of poverty.

22. Miller, 571, makes this point

23. John Kenneth Galbraith, *The Nature of Mass Poverty*, (Cambridge and London: Harvard University, 1979), 17–20.

24. This is one of the key points made by Michael Lipton, *Why People Stay Poor: Urban Bias in World Development*, (Cambridge: Harvard University, 1977).

25. This view is common in the literature. A short explanation of it in terms of education can be found in Kenneth Kehrer, "Education, Race and Poverty," in *Perspectives on Poverty*, Dennis J. Dugan and William H. Leahy eds., (New York: Praeger, 1973), 31–42 and particularly 32–33.

26. Galbraith ibid., 17–18. Note Galbraith's use of psychological terms here, this becomes important later.

27. Miller, ibid., 575–576.

28. The term was popularized by Oscar Lewis in "The Culture of Poverty," *Scientific American* 1966. 215. 19–25.

29. Theodore R. Sarbin, "The Culture of Poverty, Social Identity and Cognitive Outcomes," in *Psychological Factors in Poverty*, Vernon L. Allen ed., (Chicago: Markham 1970), 32.

30. Ibid., 33.

31. Ibid., 34.

32. Ibid., 34–35.

33. Richard N. Farmer, *Benevolent Aggression: The Necessary Impact of the Advanced Nations on Indigenous Peoples*, (New York: David McKay, 1972), 82.

34. It is probably safe to say that primary and secondary education is available to Native American students. Though college education may be less readily available, the differences in high school graduation rates remain. In addition, it is safe to say that the high school graduation rates negatively affect college attendance.

35. George J. Mouly, *Psychology for Effective Teaching* 2nd edition, (London and New York: Holt Rinehart and Winston Inc., 1968), 567.

36. N. L. Gage and David C. Berliner, *Educational Psychology*, (Chicago: Rand McNally College Publishing Company, 1975), 282.

37. Anita E. Woolfolk, *Educational Psychology* 4th Edition, (New Jersey: Prentice Hall, 1990), 306.

38. Jon Reyhner, ed. *Teaching American Indian Students.* (Norman and London: University of Oklahoma Press, 1992), 13.

39. Indian Health Service, *Trends in Indian Health,* Ibid., 5. These figures, indeed all of the figures taken from *Trends in Indian Health* are overly conservative, as reported in U.S.Indian Health Service, *Regional Differences in Indian Health,* (Washington D.C.: Department of Health and Human Services, Division of Program Statistics, 1994), p 5. In reviewing data by region, the IHS found that the Oklahoma, California and Portland region statistics were skewed by underreporting of Indian race on death certificates. Such underreporting has the effect of lowering statistical mortality rates. If these regions are removed from calculation, the alcoholism death rate jumps to 630 percent that of the general populace and all the other mortality rates take similar jumps. The lower rates cited herein from *Trends in Indian Health* were chosen because they represent the lowest possible figures.

40. Analysis of data presented in Ibid., 46–50.

41. Robert F. Berkhofer, Jr., *The White Man's Indian,* (New York: Vintage Books, 1979), 30, notes that if there is a third major White image of the Indian after the contradictory Noble/Savage stereotypes then a "...degraded, often drunken, Indian constitutes the essence of that understanding."

42. D. Fenna, et al., "Ethanol Metabolism in Various Racial Groups", *Canadian Medical Association Journal* 105 (1971), 472–475.

43. Phillip A. May, "The Epidemiology of Alcohol Abuse," *American Indian Culture and Research Journal,* v 18, n 2 (1994), 122–123

44. Margaret M. Gallaher, et al., "Pedestrian and Hypothermia Deaths Among Native Americans in New Mexico," *Journal of the American Medical Association,* v 267, n 10 (1992), 1345–1348.

45. Carol Chiago Lujan, "Alcohol-related Deaths of American Indians, Stereotypes and Strategies," *Journal of the American Medical Association,* v 267 n 10 (1992), 1384.

46. Though there certainly are differences in drinking style which exacerbate the problem. See Deborah Jones-Saumty, Larry Hochhaus, Ralph Dru and Arthur Zeiner, "Psychological factors of Familial Alcoholism in American Indians and Caucasians," *Journal of Clinical Psychology,* (Brandon VT: Clinical Psychology Publishing Company), v 39, n 5, 1983 and Ray Stratton, Arthur Zeiner and Alfonso Paredes, "Tribal Affiliation and Prevalence of Alcohol Problems," *Journal of Studies on Alcohol,* (New Brunswick: Publication Division of the Rutgers Center of Alcohol Studies), v 39, n 7, 1978.

47. Richard Swinson and Derek Eaves, *Alcoholism and Addiction,* (London: Woburn Press, 1978), 77.

48. Gary G. Forrest., *The Diagnosis and Treatment of Alcoholism,* (Springfield: Charles C. Thomas Publisher) revised, 2nd ed. 1978. As quoted in his *Alcoholism and Human Sexuality,* (Springfield: Charles C. Thomas Publisher, 1983), 366.

49. Deborah Jones-Saumty, et. al, 788.

50. David Caster and Oscar Parsons, "Locus of Control in Alcoholics and Treatment Outcomes," *Journal of Studies on Alcohol,* (New Brunswick: Rutgers Center of Alcohol Studies), v 38, n 11, 1977, 2093 and passim.

51. Deborah Jones-Saumty, et. al.,787.

CHAPTER TWO
Settler Imperialism

> *On this land there is a great deal of timber, pine and oak, that are of much use to the white man. They send it to foreign countries and it brings them a great deal of money.*
>
> *On this land there is grass for cattle and horses and much food for hogs.*
>
> *On this land there is a great deal of tobacco raised, which likewise gives them money. Even the streams are valuable to the white man, to grind the wheat and corn he grows on his land. The pine trees that are dead are valuable for tar.*
>
> *We are told that our lands are of no service to us...*
>
> *We are afraid if we part with much more of our lands the white people will not let us keep as much as will be sufficient to bury our dead.*
>
> —Doublehead, Creek Chief[1]

The most charitable characterization of United States' law and policy concerning the Indians is paternalistic; the least that it is attempted genocide. The interplay of forces that shaped the policy included both base and noble, though more often than not the noble sentiments were obscured by parochialism or even racism. This chapter and the three that follow it will not attempt an overview of all elements of Federal Indian law and policy. That would be too ambitious and is unnecessary. For the purposes of this book, those policies that may have brought about conditions leading to the ills outlined in the Chapter One are the ones that will be examined. To help place the policies in context and to prepare for conclusion, we'll also look at the stated reasons for these policies. Where possible, competent U.S. Government authorities will be cited at length. This ensures that the extended argument so developed will be the most effective. If the policies and outcomes are described by the U.S. officials involved, then it will be hard for modern American readers to ignore the evidence. Since a link has been made between decreased self-governance and the many problems faced by modern Natives, self-governance and the broader issue of sovereignty will be a key. To the extent that the policies were unjust or genocidal, they will constitute elements of further arguments to be completed in the final chapter.

In examining the history, particular emphasis will be placed on the history of the so-called "Five Civilized Tribes" more commonly termed "The Five Tribes" today. These are the Choctaw, Chickasaw, Creek, Seminole and Cherokee nations. Though the author's Choctaw citizenship plays a role in this, there are independent reasons as well. Chief among these is the length of their struggle for sovereignty in the wake of U.S. independence. The fourth U.S. treaty with any Indian nation was with the Cherokee, the fifth and sixth with the Choctaw and Chickasaw respectively; all concluded before the enactment of the United States Constitution. They were the last Indian nations in the 48 contiguous states to be forcibly included into a state, the state of Oklahoma. They continue their fight for sovereignty to this day. The history of their interaction with the United States Government thus spans the history of the United States itself and includes all major elements of U.S. policy concerning Indian nations.

Most American commentators call the earliest era of U.S. policy "assimilation," though this more nearly characterizes the hopes of U.S. policymakers rather than the actual results of their policies. With the spirit of the enlightenment, believing their new government to be truly superior, the founders of the United States thought that the Indians would willingly join them. Until then, in the words of Jefferson, "... the Indians had the full, undivided and independent sovereignty as long as they choose to keep it, and that this might be forever."[2] Thus from the earliest days of the republic, such luminaries as Jefferson fully recognized Indian sovereignty in no uncertain terms, however no one seriously believed that the Indian nations would maintain their independence once the benefits of "civilization" were known to them. To this end the United States engaged in relatively non-coercive trade and education during this period. Though governmental policy was supposedly one of freely-chosen assimilation, the citizens of the United States pursued their own ends in direct conflict to official policy. Their unofficial "policy" might best be termed "settler imperialism." Like assimilation, settler imperialism had its roots in the American Revolution.

The causes of the American Revolution aren't just taxation, representation, or a desire for democracy. Perhaps paramount was

Settler Imperialism

the desire to take land held by Indians. Two crucial elements came together to bring about the desire to overthrow British rule. One was the Treaty of 1763 ending the war with France; the other is the Proclamation Line of 1763.

> The importance of the Treaty of 1763 was at once American and Atlantic, continental and maritime. The French Empire in North America had come to an end; in Canada English culture and institutions came to dominate, but never quite swamp, the French; and British North America was more than doubled in extent, although the *habitants* numbered only some seventy-five thousand. . . . Britain no longer needed to make concessions, and the colonies for their part developed wills of their own. The paths to the West now seemed open to them.... The American Revolution has its origins in the oversuccessful terms of the Treaty of 1763.[3]

The second element, the Proclamation Line of 1763, was the last obstacle to westward expansion. King George III set up the line as the official boundary dividing the English colonies and the Indian nations. Prior to this, relations between the British and the various Indian nations had grown steadily worse. Colonists constantly intruded into Native held land and the Indian nations responded by attacking British settlements. The war with the French had been longer and more costly than necessary because the French had more support among the Indian nations. With the end of the war, the King sought to end the ongoing strife with the Indian nations.[4] While it might be profitable for the colonists to take the Indian land, it was very unprofitable for the crown whose troops had to protect the colonists. The Proclamation Line of 1763 was thus a major irritant to the colonists who sought to expand the frontier.

> The frontier represented America's imperialism and, like all settler imperialisms, it was rough and ready in its methods, antinative in its essence, and scornful of the liberal but remote control of London. The liberty it sought in the West was liberty to take Indian property without too much fuss, an imperialism that did not cease with 1776.[5]

Settler imperialism was to be the practical form of U.S. policy toward Native Americans from 1776 to at least the 1830's. Just like the British Government before them, the U.S. Government attempted to minimize its losses by maintaining peace despite the pressure of settlers hungry for Indian lands. The United States Government negotiated over one-hundred treaties in this era.[6] Each one set out boundaries; guaranteed safety and protection of Indian people and property; and either implicitly or explicitly recognized the sovereignty of the Indian signatories. Despite this, the citizens of the United States openly violated the agreements. After 1789, with the U.S. Constitution and Government in place, this practice can be easily traced by examining official pronouncements of the President. One of the first is in a letter from George Washington to the United States Senate. It mentions earlier abuses; lays out the culpability of U.S. citizens and the responsibility of the United States to punish those citizens; and offers the alternative that the United States might compensate the Indians for land taken by settlers. It reads in part:

> During the last year I laid before the Senate a particular statement of the case of the Cherokees. By a reference to that paper it will appear that the United States formed a treaty with the Cherokees in November, 1785; that the said Cherokees thereby placed themselves under the protection of the United States and had a boundary assigned them; that the white people settled on the frontiers had openly violated the said boundary by intruding on the Indian lands; that the United States in Congress assembled did, on the 1st day of September, 1788, issue their proclamation forbidding all such unwarrantable intrusions, and enjoined all those who had settled upon the hunting grounds of the Cherokees to depart with their families and effects without loss of time, as they would answer their disobedience to the injunctions and prohibitions expressed at their peril.
>
> But information has been received that notwithstanding the said treaty and proclamation upward of 500 families have settled on the Cherokee lands exclusively of those settled between the fork of French Broad and Holstein rivers, mentioned in the said treaty.
>
> As the obstructions to a proper conduct on this matter have been removed since it was mentioned to the Senate on the 22d of August, 1789, by the accession of North Carolina to the present Union and the cessions of the land in question, I shall conceive myself bound to exert the powers intrusted [sic] to me by the Constitution in order to carry into faithful execution the treaty of Hopewell, unless it shall be thought proper to attempt to

arrange a new boundary with the Cherokees, embracing the settlements, and compensating the Cherokees for the cessions they shall make on the occasion.[7]

The intrusions and subsequent purchases of land continued apace throughout this era. They can be traced through the Presidential Proclamation of 26 August, 1790;[8] Presidential Proclamation of 19 March, 1791;[9] President Washington's Fourth Annual Address of 6 November, 1792;[10] and a particularly terrible episode recorded in this Presidential Proclamation:

> Whereas I have received authentic information that certain lawless and wicked persons of the western frontier in the State of Georgia did lately invade, burn, and destroy a town belonging to the Cherokee Nation, although in amity with the United States, and put to death several Indians of that nation; and
>
> Whereas such outrageous conduct not only violates the rights of humanity, but also endangers the public peace, and it highly becomes the honor and good faith of the United States to pursue all legal means for the punishment of those atrocious offenders:
>
> I have therefore thought fit to issue this my proclamation, hereby exhorting all the citizens of the United States and requiring all the officers thereof, according to their respective stations, to use their utmost endeavors to apprehend and bring those offenders to justice. And I do moreover offer a reward of $500 for each and every of the above-named persons who shall be so apprehended and brought to justice and shall be proved to have assumed or exercised any command or authority among the perpetrators of the crimes aforesaid at the time of committing the same.
>
> In testimony whereof I have caused the seal of the United States to be affixed to these presents, and signed the same with my hand. Done at the city of Philadelphia, the 12th day of December. A.D. 1792, and of the Independence of the United States the seventeenth. [SEAL.] *signed* George Washington.[11]

Further evidence is contained in a Letter to Congress of 17 February 1795,[12] Letter to the Senate of 25 June 1795,[13] Letter to Congress of 8 December, 1795,[14] and the 2nd Annual Address of 8 December 1798.[15] A particularly interesting letter was sent to congress by Thomas Jefferson on the 18th of January, 1803. In part it says:

The Indian tribes residing within the limits of the United States have for a considerable time been growing more and more uneasy at the constant diminution of the territory they occupy, although effected by their own voluntary sales, and the policy has long been gaining strength with them of refusing absolutely all further sale on any conditions, insomuch that at this time it hazards their friendship and excites dangerous jealousies and perturbations in their minds to make any overture for the purchase of the smallest portions of their land. A very few tribes only are not yet obstinately in these dispositions.[16]

Though many of the sales of territory had been prompted directly by the settler imperialism of the United States, and probably all were influenced by it, Jefferson nevertheless calls the sales "voluntary." Indian voluntarism is a theme repeated in various circumstances throughout the history of U.S. Indian policy. The Indian nations are given a choice between two evils, like loss of territory versus death and destruction by settlers with a concomitant loss of territory anyway. When they choose to cede territory, it is a "voluntary cession." That the Indian nations should be adamant in refusal to sell further land, as admitted by Jefferson, gives lie to the supposed voluntary nature of the transaction.

Though the Indian nations and individuals of those nations were regularly engaged in hostilities with the White settlers, they usually did so in response to provocation admitted by the President of the United States. In only two instances during this era did the President insinuate that there might not have been provocation. George Washington did so concerning tribes north of the Ohio River in his 2nd Annual Address on December 8th, 1790[17] and James Madison did so concerning some southern tribes in his 7th Annual Address of December 5th, 1815.[18] Thus it would seem that the Indian nations, on the whole, attempted to get along with their American neighbors.

Despite the fact that the Federal Government lacked the will to enforce its own treaties, it was not completely without principle. The U.S. Government was aware almost from the start that the treaties were insufficient to stem the tide of intruders. In an attempt to stop settler imperialism and advance the cause of assimilation, Congress passed a series of acts known as the Trade and Intercourse Acts.[19] Given that the U.S. Government was unable to enforce the treaties, it should be clear that stacking up even more laws toward the same end would result in just that many more unenforceable laws. It did. Most of the incursions already cited occurred after the Trade and Intercourse Acts were law. Though the Trade and Intercourse Acts cannot be called a complete failure, by the 1830's most of the Indian nations in the eastern portion of the United States were surrounded. In 1819 the situation was so serious that the Civilization Fund Act was passed in part to prevent the "final extinction of Indian tribes, adjoining the frontier settlements of the United States. . . ."[20]

Why did settler imperialism win despite what seems like sincere concern and outrage on the part of some of the top policymakers in the U.S.? Political expediency, racism, elitism and practical matters of implementation all seem to have played a part. A crucial element in the failure of U.S. law was the fact that it immediately arrogated unto itself the right to try and punish Whites that had transgressed.[21] But, as Prucha put it, "The typical frontier community could not be brought to convict a man who injured or murdered an Indian..."[22] This combined with the fact that the Indians were often not allowed into court meant that even if an arrest was made, the white man would usually go free.

But far fewer were arrested than might be thought. It is probable that local police were almost as biased as the juries. Since the statutes and treaties were often enforced in war-like situations, it frequently fell to military formations to provide the enforcement. Here the history and principles of the United States worked against enforcement. The United States still mistrusted the notion of a standing Army, so most of the U.S. military was state militia. But the militia, often drawn from the very settlers who were perpetrating the crimes, were of little value in enforcing the rules. George Washington may be alluding to this in a 1797 letter to the House of Representatives calling for troops to enforce agreements with the Indian nations,

> It is generally agreed that some cavalry, either militia or regular, will be necessary; and according to the best information I have been able to obtain, it is my opinion that the latter will be less expensive and more useful than the former in preserving peace. . . .[23]

Whether he was referring to the bias of the militia, or to its general ineffectiveness probably can never be known. Either way, the militia were to be the main enforcers of the Indian boundaries despite their ineffectiveness.

The Congress passed laws and enacted treaties that the settlers wouldn't obey because they were two very different groups of people with divergent interests. The legislators were all landholders, mostly wealthy. Many were well-versed in enlightenment philosophy, allowing them to consider the ethics of their actions and the rights of the Native Americans. Their relative wealth meant that they could afford the courage of their convictions. The landless immigrants that became settlers were scarcely enlightenment philosophers. They had come to the America for land, and they meant to get it. In an age when racism was so normal that there wasn't even a word for it, it is not surprising that the settlers chose their own welfare over that of another people. Though some might respect the laws and treaties of the United States, the ineffectiveness of U.S. Government enforcement meant that the settlers didn't *have to* respect them. Ultimately the settler's desire for land and their lack of scruples in taking it ensured that settler imperialism would win out.

The tribes generally continued a friendly policy despite a steady diminution of their land. Even so, there was a constant pressure for more land that could not be sated. Events like the Louisiana Purchase seemed to solve the land problem by providing enough land for any influx of settlers. However, more thoughtful minds realized that the entire area purchased contained Indian nations which, whatever their relative population density, occupied the territory. That policymakers were aware of the Indian nations within the purchased territory and recognized their right to self-government is laid out in Jefferson's 3rd Annual Message of 1803:

> With the wisdom of Congress it will rest to take those ulterior measures which may be necessary for the immediate occupation and temporary government of the country; for its incorporation into our Union; for rendering the change of government a blessing to our newly adopted brethren; for securing to them the rights of conscience and of property; for confirming to the Indian inhabitants their occupancy and self-government, establishing friendly and commercial relations with them, and for ascertaining the geography of the country acquired. Such materials, for your information, relative to its affairs in general as the short space of time has permitted me to collect will be laid before you when the subject shall be in a state for your consideration.[24]

Thus the Louisiana Purchase, for the remainder of the assimilation era, just meant a larger realm for settler imperialism to work on while the U.S. Government ineffectually attempted to enforce the increasing number of treaties that were supposed to guarantee the integrity of the Indian nations.

Though white settlers almost continuously violated the treaties between the U.S. Government and the governments of the various Indian nations, the Indian nations continued to negotiate treaties in the vain hope that the United States would finally enforce one. The consternation among the Indian nations is difficult to express. Not only were they being forced into smaller and smaller lands, but this was happening in direct contradiction to treaties. This was unthinkable.

The fact that Indian nations could not conceive of the breaking of a treaty may explain why they continued to negotiate despite mounting evidence that such negotiations were futile. As Robert Williams Jr. explains, Indian nations consider treaties to be sacred texts, establishing a connection between the parties.[25] Virtually every treaty negotiated from the founding of the United States up until the 1830's specifically speaks of "friendship" between the parties. Two treaties, one before[26] and one after[27] 1830 go so far as to call the Whites "brothers." The Indian nations clearly thought that they were being guaranteed a relationship of mutual trust and good-will in which the parties were on an equal footing. These treaties were meant not just to guarantee the boundaries between the nations, but to establish a mutuality in which neither side was subservient to the other. In short, these treaties did not just implicitly recognize the sovereignty of the Indian nations, but from an Indian perspective were a clear guarantee of their continued sovereignty.

The U.S. Government's failure to enforce its treaties had allowed the Indian nations in the east to be completely surrounded, threatening not just their sovereignty but their very existence. The remaining land was scarcely sufficient for the eastern Indian nations to survive. Continued pressure for new land and a growing desire for what might be called "territorial integrity" led some state governments to pressure the Federal Government for the complete removal of Indians from their state. As early as 1802,[28] Georgia had entered into an agreement with the Federal Government in which the Federal Government was to purchase the remaining Indian land in Georgia. Unfortunately the Indian nations of the east, and particularly those in

Georgia, would not sell the little land remaining to them.

Indian refusal to sell their land and the insatiable settler appetite for more land was an explosive combination. With their existence threatened, the Indian nations in the east might fight. The drive for territorial integrity and the natural overland westward expansion of settlers meant that the new settlers were not going to skip over the Indian territory left in the east, to take the land west of the Mississippi. Besides, the land west of the Mississippi was already occupied by Indian nations. The natural solution from the settler perspective was to remove the eastern Indian nations, concentrating the Indian nations on land west of the Mississippi. Removal would open up land for immediate settlement and provide territorial integrity.

Though many looked to removal as a solution, there was no straightforward legal grounds under existing U.S. law to force the Indians to sell their lands and move west. Thus the inexorability of the settler demand for land meant that the United States Government would soon be faced with a number of equally unattractive possibilities. If it failed to enforce its laws and treaties, the settlers would provoke full-scale war with the Indian nations. Losing such a war was out of the question; while winning meant the deaths of the Indian nations the U.S. had solemnly sworn to protect. On the other hand, enforcement of the laws and treaties would be tantamount to civil war because the states and settlers wouldn't stand for it. Removal was the only possible answer, the question was how to accomplish it.

Notes

1. As quoted by Nerburn, Kent and Louise Mengelkoch, editors, *Native American Wisdom. The Classic Wisdom Collection*, (San Rafael CA: New World Library, 1991), 51–52.

2. As quoted by Francis Paul Prucha, *American Indian Policy in the Formative Years: The Trade and Intercourse Acts, 1790–1834*, (Cambridge: Harvard University, 1962),141.

3. Esmond Wright ,"Fabric of Freedom 1763-1800" in *The Making of America*, David Donald ed., (London: Macmillan, 1965), 2.

4. Francis Paul Prucha, *The Great Father*, (Bison Books paperback combined and unabridged volumes 1 and 2 edition, 1995; Lincoln and

London: University of Nebraska, 1984), 21–28.

5. Wright,. 44.

6. See Appendix D for a set of particularly explicit treaty excerpts. Most of these date from after the assimilation era, primarily because Indian nations did not demand explicit recognition of their prerogatives until after these had been ignored a number of times. However, the over one-hundred treaties of the assimilation era all implicitly recognize sovereignty, independence, government, laws and jurisdiction of Indian nations.

7. James Richardson ed., *Messages and Papers of the Presidents*, (Washington: Bureau of National Literature, 1911) v 1, p 71.

8. Ibid., 72–73

9. Ibid., 93–94.

10. Ibid., 119.

11. Ibid., 129.

12. Ibid., 167.

13. Ibid., 171.

14. Ibid., 174 and 177.

15. Ibid., 264.

16. Ibid., 341.

17. Ibid., 74. However, Washington's protestations appear have been a rationalization for subduing the Indian nations in the area so that the war debt from the revolution could be met by the sale of land in the area. For a complete account, see Wiley Sword, *President Washington's Indian War: The Struggle for the Old Northwest 1790–1795*, (Norman and London: University of Oklahoma, 1985).

18. Ibid., 548.

19. For the texts of the first and last of these acts, in 1790 and 1802, see Francis Paul Prucha ed., *Documents of United States Indian Policy*, 2nd expanded edition, (Lincoln and London: University of Nebraska, 1990). 14–15, 17–21.

20. *U.S. Statutes at Large*, 3:5 16.

21. Though some tribes were recognized by treaty as having a right to punish white people, for example the Choctaw as stated in Article 4 of, TREATY WITH THE CHOCTAW {1786, Jan. 3} 7 Stat., 21, this was uncommon. In addition, exercise of such right was apt to create a backlash.

22. Prucha, *Great Father*, 105.

23. James Richardson, 204.

24. Ibid., 346–347.

25. Robert A. Williams, Jr.. *Linking Arms Together: American Indian Treaty Visions of Law and Peace, 1600–1800* (New York and London: Routledge, 1999) provides the most complete discussion of the American Indian view of treaties, their significance and goals during this period. The

second chapter of this book is entitled, "Treaties as Sacred Texts," while the third chapter is entitled "Treaties as Connections." Though some of his conclusions only apply to the period 1600–1800, the notion of treaty as sacred text continues to this day.

26. TREATY WITH THE CHEROKEE {1816, Mar. 22}, 7 Stat., 138. Ratified Apr. 8, 1816.

27. TREATY WITH THE CHICKASAW {1834, May 24}, 7 Stat., 450. Proclamation, July 1, 1834

28. J. E. Hays, ed., *Indian Treaties: Cessions of Land in Georgia 1705–1837,* (W.P.A. Project No. 7158, 1941), 332–334.

CHAPTER 3
Removal

> *The man who said that he would plant a stake and draw a line around us, that never should be passed, was the first to say that he could not guard the lines, and drew up the stake and wiped out all traces of the line. I will not conceal from you my fears, that the present grounds may be removed. I have my foreboding,—who of us can tell after witnessing what has already been done, what the next force may be.*
> —George W. Harkins, District Chief
> of the Choctaw Nation, 1833[1]

No amount of pressure seemed sufficient to force the eastern tribes to remove. Somehow, additional pressure would have to be brought to bear. The ongoing treaty relationship between the U.S. and the Indian nations, though never a reliable guarantor of Indian safety, did serve to diminish the threat of settler imperialism. If the United States could repudiate its treaties, then the threat would be ratcheted up significantly. But the United States couldn't just repudiate its treaties, that would expose the dubious legal and moral ground that the nation was standing on, as well as the base motives behind their stand. It would instead engage in what David Wilkins has called "masking."[2] It would spin a web of contradicting laws, policies, theories and myths that after seventy years would culminate in the assertion of a legal right, sometimes even a duty, to repudiate Indian treaties. The immediate effect would be to diminish the force of the treaties, making the hopes of enforcement even slimmer than before. In this way, the eastern Indian nations might be forced to remove.

All three branches of the Federal Government would be involved in forcing removal. The Supreme Court would provide the legal underpinnings which would allow removal as well as advancing various rationales for diminishing the status of the relationship between the U.S. and the Indian nations; the Presidency, long held by idealists, would finally be held by a President willing pervert the original intent of laws protecting Indian nations to the extent that he could assert a duty *not* to protect them in certain cases; and the Congress would codify removal as an official policy despite its seeming contradiction of existing laws and treaties.

A series of Supreme Court decisions provided the framework for removal and continue to be central to understanding U.S. Indian Law to this day. The first of these, *Johnson v. McIntosh* of 1823, laid out the legal framework for the taking of Indian lands.

> On the discovery of this immense continent the great nations of Europe were eager to appropriate to themselves so much of it as they could respectively acquire. Its vast extent offered ample field to the ambition and enterprise of all; and the character and religion of its inhabitants afforded an apology for considering them as a people over whom the superior genius of Europe might claim an ascendancy. The potentates of the old world found no difficulty in convincing themselves that they made ample compensation to the inhabitants of the new, by bestowing on them civilization and Christianity, in exchange for unlimited independence. But, as they were all in pursuit of nearly the same object, it was necessary, in order to avoid conflicting settlements and consequent war with each other, to establish a principle, which all should acknowledge as the law by which the right of acquisition, which they all asserted, should be regulated between themselves. This principle was, that discovery gave title to the government by whose subjects, or by whose authority, it was made, against all other European governments, which title might be consummated by possession . . .
>
> Thus, all the nations of Europe, who have acquired territory on this continent, have asserted in themselves, and have recognized in others, the exclusive right of the discoverer to appropriate the lands occupied by the Indians. Have the American States rejected or adopted this principle? . . .
>
> The United States then have unequivocally conceded to that great and broad rule by which its civilized inhabitants now hold this country. They hold, and assert in themselves, the title by which it was acquired. They maintain, as all others have maintained, that discovery gave an exclusive right to extinguish the

Indian title of occupancy, either by purchase or by conquest . . .

We will not enter into the controversy, whether agriculturists, merchants, and manufacturers, have a right, on abstract principles, to expel hunters from the territory they possess, or to contract their limits. Conquest gives a title which the courts of the conqueror cannot deny, whatever the private and speculative opinions of individuals may be, respecting the original justice of the claim which has been successfully asserted . . . These claims have been maintained and established as far west as the river Mississippi, by the sword . . .

When the conquest is complete, and the conquered inhabitants can be blended with the conquerors, or safely governed as a distinct people, public opinion, which not even the conqueror can disregard imposes these restraints on him . . .

But the Indians inhabiting this country were fierce savages . . . [T]o govern them as a distinct people, was impossible, because they were as brave and as high spirited as they were fierce, and were ready to repel by arms every attempt on their independence.

What was the inevitable consequence of this state of things? The Europeans were under the necessity of either abandoning the country, and relinquishing their pompous claims to it, or of enforcing those claims by the sword, and by the adoption of principles adapted to the condition of people with whom it was impossible to mix, and who could not be governed as a distinct society, or of remaining in their neighborhood, and exposing themselves and their families to the perpetual hazard of being massacred.

Frequent and bloody wars in which the whites were not always the aggressors, unavoidably ensued . . .

However extravagant the pretension of converting the discovery of a country into conquest may appear; if it has been asserted in the first instance, and afterwards sustained; if a country has been acquired and held under it; if the property of the great mass of the community originates in it, it becomes the law of the land, and cannot be questioned . . . However this restriction may be opposed to natural right, and to the usages of civilized nations, yet, if it be indispensable to that system under which the country has been settled, and be adapted to the actual condition of the two people, it may, perhaps, be supported by reason, and certainly cannot be rejected by Courts of justice.[3]

The U.S. Government then, had a right under the "doctrine of discovery," to take Indian land by purchase or by conquest. It stipulates that the territory as far west as the river Mississippi had been won "by the sword,"[4] recognizing that the Whites were usually the aggressors, but merely because the Indians were "ready to repel by arms every attempt on their independence." This remarkable opinion even recognizes the dubious moral ground that the United States was standing on. Almost explicitly invoking the notion that "ought implies can," Marshall asserts that settler imperialism cannot be stopped and thus will be institutionalized. The one mitigating factor is that only the Federal Government can exercise the power, since the right of discovery has devolved on the Federal Government and only they can declare war.

The U.S. Government, via the doctrine of discovery, claims the legal right to conquer Indian nations to take their land. The only alternative open to Indian nations under this doctrine is to sell their land. Thus any U.S. purchase from 1823 onward must be seen as coercive. Despite the license given in *Johnson v. McIntosh,* the U.S. would not force sales until the Jackson Presidency and not even openly then. As late as 1824, a year *after* the U.S. had claimed the legal right to take Indian land, President Monroe would not make use of it. As he remarked in a letter to Congress concerning Georgia's demands that the U.S. live up to its compact of 1802 and extinguish remaining Indian title in Georgia,

> The express stipulation of the compact that their title should be extinguished at the expense of the United States when it may be done peaceably and on reasonable conditions is a full proof that it was the clear and distinct understanding of both parties to it that the Indians had a right to the territory, in the disposal of which they were to be regarded as free agents. An attempt to remove them by force would, in my opinion, be unjust.[5]

Even so Monroe himself laid the ground for the rationale that allows Jackson to implement removal, and in addition foreshadows the later allotment policy in his 2nd Inaugural Address of March 5th 1821,

> The care of the Indian tribes within our limits has long been an essential part of our system, but, unfortunately, it has not been executed in a manner to accomplish all the objects intended by it. We have treated them as independent nations, without

their having any substantial pretensions to that rank. The distinction has flattered their pride, retarded their improvement, and in many instances paved the way to their destruction. The progress of our settlements westward, supported as they are by a dense population, has constantly driven them back, with almost the total sacrifice of the lands which they have been compelled to abandon. They have claims on the magnanimity and, I may add, on the justice of this nation which we must all feel. We should become their real benefactors; we should perform the office of their Great Father, the endearing title which they emphatically give to the Chief Magistrate of our Union. Their sovereignty over vast territories should cease, in lieu of which the right of soil should be secured to each individual and his posterity in competent portions; and for the territory thus ceded by each tribe some reasonable equivalent should be granted, to be vested in permanent funds for the support of civil government over them and for the education of their children, for their instruction in the arts of husbandry, and to provide sustenance for them until they could provide it for themselves. My earnest hope is that Congress will digest some plan, founded on these principles, with such improvements as their wisdom may suggest, and carry it into effect as soon as it may be practicable.[6]

Though clearly providing a rationale for the dissolution of the Indian nations, Monroe did not avail himself of the option. Indeed, as late as April 12th, 1824 in his 7th Annual Message to Congress he would write,

My impression is equally strong that it would promote essentially the security and happiness of the tribes within our limits if they could be prevailed on to retire west and north of our States and Territories on lands to be procured for them by the United States, in exchange for those on which they now reside. Surrounded as they are, and pressed as they will be, on every side by the white population, it will be difficult if not impossible for them, with their kind of government, to sustain order among them. Their interior will be exposed to frequent disturbance to remedy which the interposition of the United States will be indispensable, and thus their government will gradually lose its authority until it is annihilated. In this process the moral character of the tribes will also be lost, since the change will be too rapid to admit their improvement in civilization to enable them to institute and sustain a government founded on our principles, if such a change were compatible either with the compact with Georgia or with our general system, or to become members of a State, should any State be willing to adopt them in such numbers, regarding the good order, peace, and tranquillity of such State. But all these evils may be avoided if these tribes will consent to remove beyond the limits of our present States and Territories. Lands equally good, and perhaps more fertile, may be procured for them in those quarters. The relations between the United States and such Indians would still be the same.[7]

Between these two documents we can see the sense of futility engendered in some policymakers by the failure of assimilation; the sense that they will have to abandon their idealism and their great reluctance to do so. In the first Monroe entertains the actual dissolution of the tribes, claiming they have no "pretensions" to the rank of independent nation though he recognizes that they "have sovereignty over vast territories." In the second, Monroe's idealism is reasserted. He seems to recognize that there is not pretense, that they are independent nations. He explicitly recognizes that the Indian nations have governments, though he believes that the U.S. Government is superior and should be the model for Indian nations. In the end, he is resigned to removal because he does not believe the press of white settlers will allow the time for any other solution. This administration and the next would create treaties with tribes in which they would be traded lands to the west in the hope that they would remove there of their own free will, even though at this juncture such a move could hardly be called "free." States with large settler populations were quite hostile both through the actions of the state government and through the independent actions of the settlers themselves. Yet despite this coercion, the tribes resisted.

Unwillingness to force removal would continue through the Adams administration, despite the seeming license given in *Johnson v. McIntosh*. Pressure continued for decisive action, but the President could not be brought to willfully break treaties. Intrusions into Indian territory continued, particularly in Georgia, with the people of that state acting openly to bring the Indian nations into their jurisdiction even to the extent of sending surveyors into Indian territory. In an 1827 letter to Congress, Adams acted to prevent violence and maintain the integrity of the treaties, almost pleading with the Indians to forego self-defense knowing that the

Georgians would use any violence on the part of non-whites as a pretense for open war.

> Instructions have accordingly been given by the Secretary of War to the attorney and marshal of the United States in the district of Georgia to commence prosecutions against the surveyors complained of as having violated the law, while orders have at the same time been forwarded to the agent of the United States at once to assure the Indians that their rights founded upon the treaty and the law are recognized by this Government and will be faithfully protected, and earnestly to exhort them, by the forbearance of every act of hostility on their part, to preserve unimpaired that right to protection secured to them by the sacred pledge of the good faith of this nation. Copies of these instructions and orders are herewith transmitted to Congress.[8]

Later in the same letter, it becomes clear that this is a constitutional crisis of the highest magnitude as Adams threatens the use of force against the state of Georgia. He makes it clear that Congress can avert the crisis by changing the law, but also seems to invoke moral authority,

> In the present instance it is my duty to say that if the legislative and executive authorities of the State of Georgia should persevere in acts of encroachment upon the territories secured by a solemn treaty to the Indians, and the laws of the Union remain unaltered, a superadded obligation even higher than that of human authority will compel the Executive of the United States to enforce the laws and fulfill the duties of the nation by all the force committed for that purpose to his charge.[9]

Adams' threat of force created an uneasy stalemate that would not be broken until the Jackson presidency. Ironically, though perhaps inevitably, Andrew Jackson broke the stalemate. His Presidency was largely based on his reputation as a hero of the War of 1812 at the Battle of New Orleans. In this battle a force of Choctaws had fought alongside Jackson, living up to their treaty obligation of friendship.[10] Despite this powerful example of solemn observance of treaties well-known to him, Jackson would seek to break the treaties held with Indian nations including the Choctaw. Rationalizing removal by merging the various themes from his predecessors, the courts and the Congress as well as artfully forgetting facts long since admitted, Jackson forced removal. His general stance is laid out in these excerpts from an extended policy statement made on December 8th, 1829.

>The condition and ulterior destiny of the Indian tribes within the limits of some of our States have become objects of much interest and importance. It has long been the policy of Government to introduce among them the arts of civilization, in the hope of gradually reclaiming them from a wandering life. This policy has, however, been coupled with another wholly incompatible with its success. Professing a desire to civilize and settle them, we have at the same time lost no opportunity to purchase their lands and thrust them farther into the wilderness. By this means they have not only been kept in a wandering state, but been led to look upon us as unjust and indifferent to their fate. Thus, though lavish in its expenditures upon the subject, Government has constantly defeated its own policy, and the Indians in general, receding farther and farther to the west, have retained their savage habits. A portion, however, of the Southern tribes, having mingled much with the whites and made some progress in the arts of civilized life, have lately attempted to erect an independent government within the limits of Georgia and Alabama. These States, claiming to be the only sovereigns within their territories, extended their laws over the Indians, which induced the latter to call upon the United States for protection.
>
>Under these circumstances the question presented was whether the General Government had a right to sustain those people in their pretensions. The Constitution declares that "no new State shall be formed or erected within the jurisdiction of any other State" without the consent of its legislature. If the General Government is not permitted to tolerate the erection of a confederate State within the territory of one of the members of this Union against her consent, much less could it allow a foreign and independent government to establish itself there...
>
>Actuated by this view of the subject, I informed the Indians inhabiting parts of Georgia and Alabama that their attempt to establish an independent government would not be countenanced by the Executive of the United States, and advised them to emigrate beyond the Mississippi or submit to the laws of those States.
>
>Our conduct toward these people is deeply interesting to our national character. Their present condition, contrasted with

what they once were, makes a most powerful appeal to our sympathies. Our ancestors found them the uncontrolled possessors of these vast regions. By persuasion and force they have been made to retire from river to river and from mountain to mountain, until some of the tribes have become extinct and others have left but remnants to preserve for awhile their once terrible names. Surrounded by the whites with their arts of civilization, which by destroying the resources of the savage doom him to weakness and decay, the fate of the Mohegan, the Narragansett, and the Delaware is fast overtaking the Choctaw, the Cherokee, and the Creek. That this fate surely awaits them if they remain within the limits of the States does not admit of a doubt. Humanity and national honor demand that every effort should be made to avert so great a calamity. It is too late to inquire whether it was just in the United States to include them and their territory within the bounds of new States, whose limits they could control. That step can not be retraced. A State can not be dismembered by Congress or restricted in the exercise of her constitutional power. But the people of those States and of every State, actuated by feelings of justice and a regard for our national honor, submit to you the interesting question whether something can not be done, consistently with the rights of the States, to preserve this much-injured race.[11]

A little of the old Jeffersonian idealism remains. The failure of assimilation is blamed on the wanderings caused by constant sale of lands. The Indians just weren't in any one place long enough for the teachings to work; U.S. civilization would have taken hold otherwise. Forgetting that the U.S. has maintained government-to-government treaty relations with the Indian nations from the very first, Jackson credits the civilizing influence of the Whites with allowing the independent governments the Indians "have lately attempted to erect." In a bizarre twist, the notion that the Indians are erecting these White inspired governments is what allows Jackson to rationalize removal. The Constitution forbids the establishment of new states within old. Jackson openly wonders at the justice of allowing states to come into being with Indian nations in their midst, but like the Supreme Court, he considers it idle to speculate on history. At each step it seems, there is what justice demands and then there is what actually happens to the Indian nations. If only after the fact, the injustice is recognized. Unfortunately it is also institutionalized.

In an attempt to avoid the Georgia crisis and head-off similar problems in the future, Congress passed the Indian Removal Act of May 28, 1830.[12] It enabled the President to make arrangements for removal, but did not straightforwardly assert a right to force the Indian nations to move. It speaks of the ". . . tribes or nations of Indians as may choose to exchange the lands where they now reside, and remove there..."[13] The prod, as before, was to be the individual U.S. citizens and the state governments; and, as before, the U.S. Government was to ". . . forever secure and guaranty to them . . ."[14] their new land. The closest it comes to requiring force is in section 2,

> . . . That it shall and may be lawful for the President to exchange any or all of such districts, [western land set aside for removal] so to be laid off and described, with any tribe or nation of Indians now residing within the limits of any of the states or territories, and with which the United States have existing treaties, for the whole or any part or portion of the territory claimed and occupied by such tribe or nation, within the bounds of any one or more of the states or territories, where the land claimed and occupied by the Indians, is owned by the United States, or the United States are bound to the state within which it lies to extinguish the Indian claim thereto.[15]

Though tortuously worded, it appears that this section authorizes removal in two cases where the land is within the confines of an existing states or territories. One is when the United States already owns the land, the other is when the U.S. is bound to extinguish the Indian title. The second appears to refer to cases like that of the Georgia Compact, but speaks of the U.S. as being "bound" to "extinguish" and fails to include the original Compact's proviso that it be done peaceably. Given that *Johnson v. McIntosh* allows Indian title to be extinguished by purchase or by conquest and that the U.S. is bound to extinguish the title, it appears that this requires the government to use force if the Indians do not sell.

Perhaps most ominously, the Removal Act's guarantee that the new Indian land shall be theirs forever contains the proviso, "That such lands shall revert to the United States, if the Indians become extinct, or abandon the same."[16]

Was the U.S. bound to enforce its treaties guaranteeing the territorial integrity of Indian nations, or was it supposed to remove the Indian nations under the Removal Act? The Federal Government was the only check on the state governments and settlers who wanted to dismember the Indian nations of the east. This uncertainty put incredible pressure on the Indian nations to accept removal. The states, particularly Georgia, did everything they could to increase the pressure.

Though there was great pressure to remove, most tribes refused. Georgia continued its policy of intrusion. Though prior presidents had all but gone to war against Georgia in similar circumstances, Jackson did nothing to interfere. This prompted the Senate to require an explanation of Jackson's failure to enforce the various treaties and acts that should have prevented Georgia's actions. Jackson's February 26th, 1831 letter to the Senate reinterprets the Trade and Intercourse Act to allow his inaction.

> By the nineteenth section of this act it is provided that nothing in it "shall be construed to prevent any trade or intercourse with Indians living on lands surrounded by settlements of citizens of the United States and being within the ordinary jurisdiction of any of the individual States." This provision I have interpreted as being prospective in its operation and as applicable not only to Indian tribes which at the date of its passage were subject to the jurisdiction of any State, but to such also as should thereafter become so. To this construction of its meaning I have endeavored to conform, and have taken no step inconsistent with it. As soon, therefore, as the sovereign power of the State of Georgia was exercised by an extension of her laws throughout her limits, and I had received information of the same, orders were given to withdraw from the State the troops which had been detailed to prevent intrusion upon the Indian lands within it, and these orders were executed.[17]

Thus the same law which prompted Adams to threaten Georgia was now interpreted as allowing states to encompass Indian nations and take them into their jurisdiction, removing them from Federal protection. This not only threatened the Indian nations, but actively set at odds the requirements of treaties, laws and the Constitution. Congressmen sympathetic to the Indians or concerned with the integrity of U.S. law were not completely idle, but as always there was not enough support for decisive action against states or citizens involved in the taking of Indian land.

The ambivalence with which the United States Government enters removal is difficult to describe. It would seem that *Johnson v. McIntosh* asserts a legal right for the U.S. to take any Indian land it wishes in a straightforward war of conquest, at least until some tribes catch on to the fragility of Indian title and began to require title in fee simple. But policymakers were troubled by conscience. Even those who believed the Indians to be complete savages could not ignore the treaties and laws that were at odds with *Johnson v McIntosh*. A war of conquest was distasteful even to some of the would-be settlers.

With the Removal Act and Jackson's reinterpretation of the Trade and Intercourse Act, the Federal Government took over the imperial role using the states and settlers as a threat. The taking of land would now be a wholesale proposition with clearly laid out government authority. Though it was still driven by the settler desire for land, it was government regulated. Despite all this, it was still essentially the same process. As de Tocqueville chronicled it at the time:

> Nowadays the dispossession of the Indians is accomplished in a regular and, so to say, quite legal manner.
>
> When the European population begins to approach the wilderness occupied by a savage nation, the United States government usually sends a solemn embassy to them; the white men assemble the Indians in a great plain, and after they have eaten and drunk with them, they say: "What have you to do in the land of your fathers? Soon you will have to dig up their bones in order to live. In what way is the country you dwell in better than another? Are there not forests and marshes and prairies elsewhere than where you live, and can you live nowhere but under your own sun? Beyond these mountains that you see on the horizon, and on the other side of the lake which skirts your land to the west, there are vast countries where wild beasts are still found in abundance; sell your lands and go and live happily in those lands." That speech finished they spread before the Indians firearms, woolen clothes, kegs of brandy glass necklaces, pewter bracelets, earrings, and mirrors. If after the sight of all these riches, they still hesitate, it is hinted that they cannot refuse to consent to what is asked of them and that soon the government itself will be powerless to guarantee them the enjoyment of their rights. What can they do? Half convinced, half constrained, the Indians go off to dwell in a new wilderness, where the white men will not let them remain in peace for ten years. In this way the Americans cheaply ac-

quire whole provinces which the richest sovereigns in Europe could not afford to buy.[18]

Coerced sales preceded removal as one-by-one the tribes of the southeast and eventually other parts of the continent sold their land and removed to land in the center of the continent. The Choctaws went first, even before Jackson's failure to curb Georgia. Prior to Johnson v. McIntosh the United States had tried to induce the Choctaws to remove of their own free will, or at least under less coercion. Treaties, such as that of 1820,[19] traded western land for some of the eastern Choctaw holdings in the hopes that they would remove themselves. The trade was termed a "cession" and thus the precise nature of Choctaw title to the new land was unclear. After *Johnson v. McIntosh* the Choctaws require a treaty which gives title in fee simple under a special grant by the President; a guarantee that the land is to be theirs as long as they exist as a nation; jurisdiction and government over all people and property within their limits; a guarantee that they shall never be encompassed in any territory or state of the union; and a guarantee that no such territory or state shall ever have a right to pass laws for them.[20] The precision with which these treaty provisions answer the U.S. Government threat is unmistakable If kept, these provisions would ensure that there was no further diminution of Choctaw territory or sovereignty. It makes absolutely clear that the Choctaw Government had a complete understanding of their position under U.S. law. Though the removal treaties of some other Indian nations may be less precise, there is abundant evidence that all the nations understood some part of the threat they faced and took steps to protect themselves. In each case they must have felt, like the Choctaws, that removal guaranteed their continued sovereignty.

Though removal was gaining momentum, there was an attempt to swing the balance back to enforcement of previous laws. Jackson's rationale centered on his interpretation of the Trade and Intercourse Act and it was this interpretation that would be tested. The third branch of government, the judicial, would be called on to determine whether states could extend their jurisdiction into Indian territory as Jackson had asserted. The Cherokee, backed by numerous non-Indian individuals and groups, undertook a series of legal challenges to deny state jurisdiction. They insisted that their treaty rights precluded removal and guaranteed their self-governance with no state as overlord. Two Supreme Court cases resulted, providing the rest of the legal framework for Indian policy started in *Johnson v. McIntosh*. The first is *Cherokee Nation v. Georgia*.

> If Courts were permitted to indulge their sympathies, a case better calculated to excite them can scarcely be imagined. A people once numerous, powerful, and truly independent, found by our ancestors in the quiet and uncontrolled possession of an ample domain, gradually sinking beneath our superior policy, our arts and our arms, have yielded their land by successive treaties, each of which contain a solemn guarantee of the residue, until they retain no more of their formerly extensive territory than is deemed necessary to their comfortable subsistence. To preserve this remnant, the present application is made.
>
> Before we can look in to the merits of this case, a preliminary inquiry presents itself. Has this Court jurisdiction of the case?
>
> The third article of the constitution describes the extent of the judicial power. The second section closes an enumeration of the cases to which it is extended, with "controversies" "between a state or the citizens thereof, and foreign states, citizens, or subjects." A subsequent clause of the same section gives the Supreme Court original jurisdiction in all cases in which a state shall be a party. The party defendant may then unquestionably be sued in this Court. May the plaintiff sue in it? Is the Cherokee nation a foreign state in the sense in which that term is used in the constitution?
>
> The counsel for the plaintiffs have maintained the affirmative of this proposition with great earnestness and ability. So much of the argument as was intended to prove the character of the Cherokees as a state, as a distinct political society, separated from others, capable of managing its own affairs and governing itself, has, in the opinion of a majority of the judges, been completely successful. They have been uniformly treated as a state from the settlement of our country. The numerous treaties made with them by the United States recognize them as a people capable of maintaining the relations of peace and war, of being responsible in their political character for any violation of their engagements, or for any aggression committed on the citizens of the United States by any individual of their community. Laws have been enacted in the spirit of these treaties. The acts of our government plainly recognize

the Cherokee nation as a state, and the courts are bound by those acts.

A question of much more difficulty remains. Do the Cherokees constitute a foreign state in the sense of the constitution?

...But the relation of the Indians to the United States is marked by peculiar and cardinal distinctions which exist no where else.

The Indian territory is admitted to compose a part of the United States. ... In all our intercourse with foreign nations, in our commercial regulations, in any attempt at intercourse between Indians and foreign nations, they are considered to be within the jurisdictional limits of the United States, subject to many of those restraints which are imposed upon our own citizens. They acknowledge themselves in their treaties to be under the protection of the United States; they admit that the United States shall have the sole and exclusive right of regulating the trade with them, and managing all their affairs as they think proper...

Though the Indians are acknowledged to have an unquestionable, and heretofore, unquestioned right to the lands they occupy, until that right shall be extinguished by a voluntary cession to our government; yet it may well be doubted whether those tribes which reside within the acknowledged boundaries of the United States can, with strict accuracy, be denominated foreign nations. They may, more correctly, perhaps, be denominated domestic dependent nations. They occupy a territory to which we assert a title independent of their will, which must take effect in point of possession when their right of possession ceases. Meanwhile they are in a state of pupilage. Their relation to the United States resembles that of a ward to his guardian. ...

The court has bestowed its best attention on this question, and, after mature deliberation, the majority is of the opinion that an Indian tribe or nation within the United States is not a foreign state in the sense of the constitution, and cannot maintain an action in the courts of the United States. ...

If it be true that the Cherokee nation have rights, this is not the tribunal in which those rights are to be asserted. If it be true that wrongs have been inflicted, and that still greater wrongs are to be apprehended, this is not the tribunal which can redress the past or prevent the future.[21]

In *Cherokee Nation v. Georgia,* Marshall avoids a confrontation with the executive branch by denying that the courts have jurisdiction. However, he still tries to provide some protection for the Cherokees. Though the Cherokees are not a foreign nation and thus not in the court's jurisdiction, they are what he calls a "domestic dependent nation." This leads Marshall to advance two incompatible theses; that the Indians have responsible governments recognized by treaty, and they are in a state of "pupilage." He never explains what they are to be taught in their pupilage, though it would seem that "civilization" or perhaps "governance" were in mind despite the recognition that they had responsible government. But their denomination as "wards" to the U.S. "guardian" does provide a rationale for protecting the Indian nations independent of the requirements of treaties and laws that Jackson was creatively reinterpreting. The opening soliloquy in which Marshall examines the reasons for indulging "sympathies" points to this. The fact that two of the Justices denied that the Cherokee had any political or property rights in Georgia may also have played into this. Marshall may have been attempting to arouse the sympathies of the people for their newly created Indian "wards." If their sympathies were aroused, then Jackson might be brought to heel without prompting a constitutional crisis.

Whatever Marshall's reasons, the "guardianship" of the United States over Native Americans constituted an extension of power over them. Until *Cherokee Nation v. Georgia* the U.S. had only claimed the right to take Indian land. Now, by claiming "guardianship," it assumed preeminence and control but did not state precisely who would wield this power, nor to what end. The natural presumption would be that the guardianship was for the protection of Indians.

The opinion was not unanimous. Two Justices asserted that the Cherokee constituted a foreign nation.[22] Though many arguments were made for and against jurisdiction (some not included in the above excerpts), none were completely convincing, particularly in circumstances where this effectively denied the standard avenue for redress of violation of U.S. law: the courts.

Though there was certainly a great deal of sympathy for the Indian case, it was not enough to stop Jackson or the state of Georgia. Cherokee sympathizers engineered another case to get a definitive ruling. The third of Marshall's landmark decisions, *Worcester v. Georgia* provided a test case that could not be avoided by denying jurisdiction. A U.S. citizen, Worcester had been imprisoned under a Georgia law which extended its jurisdiction into the

Cherokee nation. Worcester sought release claiming that Georgia law could not extend into Cherokee territory. A U.S. citizen was suing a state for his release from its jail, so it was certainly within the court's jurisdiction. It also meant that the Cherokees were mainly spectators to the case that promised to determine their fate.

The decision provides an offhand answer to where the power concerning Indian nations is vested, but does not explicitly connect this power to the Indian status as wards. Complete power regarding Native nations lies with the Congress. As Marshall explains,

> ... [The Articles of Confederation] gave the United States in congress assembled the sole and exclusive right of "regulating the trade and managing all the affairs with the Indians, not members of any of the states: provided that the legislative power of any state within its own limits be not infringed or violated."
>
> The ambiguous phrases which followed the grant of power to the United States, were so construed by the states of North Carolina and Georgia as to annul the power itself.... The correct exposition of this article is rendered unnecessary by the adoption of our existing constitution. That instrument confers on congress the powers of war and peace; of making treaties, and of regulating commerce with foreign nations, and among the several states and with the Indian tribes. [emphasis in original] These powers comprehend all that is required for the regulation of our intercourse with the Indians. They are not limited by any restrictions on their free actions. The shackles imposed on this power, in the confederation, are discarded.[23]

It is interesting to note that the powers of peace, war, treaty and regulation of commerce were *all* that was required, and one might even say *allowed,* for interaction with Indians. But why make explicit that this fairly narrow set of powers may be applied to Indians, powers which Congress exercises with respect to foreign nations anyway? One reason may be that Indians were really of very little interest unless one wished to get more territory or conduct some trade. A treaty would do for obtaining land from "pliable" tribes; for "recalcitrant" tribes war and *Johnson v. McIntosh* would suffice. For conducting trade the Constitution gave Congress full power in the commerce clause. *Worcester v. Georgia* makes it clear that the powers of war, peace and treaty-making as outlined in the Constitution are specifically applicable to the Indian nations, as had always been understood. Thus between these documents, the only important reasons for dealing with Indians were covered. But it seems strange that Marshall would have delineated powers that were well-known, so it is at least possible that he outlined them rather as limitations to powers.[24] Unfortunately, by denominating the Indians as wards and stating that the restrictions on congressional actions were lifted even though strictly applicable only to the powers limited under the Confederation, Marshall left open avenues which could be used to increase control over Indian nations.

But such control was still in the future and the remainder of the decision makes it clear that, at the very least, Indian nations are considered self-governing. In particular he established this in the face of objections that treaty stipulations recognizing other sovereigns, first the British crown then the United States, meant that Indian nations' right to self-government were diminished. Regarding such a stipulation in the TREATY WITH THE CHEROKEE {1785, Nov. 28} 7 Stat., 18, Marshall writes,

> This stipulation is found in Indian treaties, generally. It was introduced into their treaties with Great Britain...
> ... The Indians perceived in this protection only what was beneficial to themselves—an engagement to punish aggressions on them. It merely bound the nation to the British crown, as a dependent ally, claiming the protection of a powerful friend and neighbor, and receiving the advantages of that protection, without involving the surrender of their national character.
> This is the true meaning of the stipulation, and is undoubtedly the sense in which it was made. Neither the British government, nor the Cherokees, ever understood it otherwise.
> The same stipulation entered into with the United States, is undoubtedly to be construed in the same manner.[25]

Regarding a similar stipulation in the TREATY WITH THE CHEROKEE {1794, June 26} 7 Stat., 43. Proclamation, Jan. 21, 1795, Marshall writes, "This relation was that of a nation claiming and receiving the protection of one more powerful; not that of individuals abandoning their national character, and submitting as subjects to the laws of a master."[26] In a more general sense Marshall writes,

> ... [T]he settled doctrine of the law of nations is, that a weak power does not surrender its independence—its right to self

government, by associating with a stronger, and taking its protection. A weak state, in order to provide for its safety, may place itself under the protection of one more powerful, without stripping itself of the right of government and ceasing to be a state. . . . At the present day, more than one state may be considered as holding its right to self government under the guarantee and protection of one or more allies.[27]

McLean's concurrence reiterates this theme,

What is a treaty? The answer is a compact formed between two nations or communities having the right of self-government...

By various treaties, the Cherokees have placed themselves under the protection of the United States: they have agreed to trade with no other people, nor to invoke the protection of any other sovereignty. But such agreements do not divest them of the right of self-government, nor destroy their capacity to enter into treaties or compacts.[28]

Thus it is clear that arguments which would use Indian recognition of U.S. sovereignty in treaties to deny Indian self-government cannot be maintained.

At least one passage by Marshall draws a direct parallel between Indian nations and other nations including those of Europe,

. . . The constitution, by declaring treaties already made, as well as those to be made, to be the supreme law of the land, has adopted and sanctioned the previous treaties with the Indian nations, and consequently admits their rank among those powers who are capable of making treaties. The words "treaty" and "nation" are words of our own language, selected in our diplomatic and legislative proceedings, by ourselves, having each a definite and well understood meaning. We have applied them to Indians, as we have applied them to the other nations of the earth. They are applied to all in the same sense.[29]

The practical ramifications of Indian tribes as nations in this passage are not clear given the contradictions of Indians as "wards" and the pre-eminent title of the United States under *Johnson v. McIntosh*. However, it certainly underscores the recognition of Indian nations as separate self-governing entities and makes clear that the treaties with them are supposed to be as solemn as those with any other nation.

The occasion for the case, the extension of Georgia laws into Cherokee territory leading to the arrest of Samuel Worcester, was won by the Cherokees. The majority decision was to release Worcester because the laws of Georgia "can have no force" within the Cherokee nation. Thus Jackson's rationale for inaction was thrown out. Despite this setback, removal forces remained implacable. Worcester was ordered released, but the court's order was not immediately enforced due to a technical loophole. Though the crisis point had been reached, no one was willing to provoke what might have been a civil war. The only alternative was for the Cherokees to remove.[31] McLean's concurrence foreshadows the practical outcome of the decision, and seems to recognize that it is part of a public policy at odds with the demands of morality,

> The exercise of the power of self-government by the Indians, within a state, is undoubtedly contemplated to be temporary. This is shown by the settled policy of the government, in the extinguishment of their title, and especially by the compact with Georgia. It is a question, not of abstract right, but of public policy. I do not mean to say, that the same moral rule which should regulate the affairs of private life, should not be regarded by communities or nations. But a sound public policy does require that the Indian tribes within our states should exchange their territories, upon equitable principles, or, eventually, consent to become amalgamated in our political communities.[32]

The Cherokees began their move to Indian Territory shortly after the decision, affirming their continued independence by removing themselves from the encroachment of Georgia.

With this ruling, settler imperialism continued apace. The Removal Act had authorized removal only of Indians then residing within the limits of a territory or state, but McLean's concurrence and the general understanding promoted by Jackson was that they had to remove or be amalgamated whenever they were surrounded. Though the removal treaties guaranteed their land and President Martin Van Buren asserted that it was a settled element of U.S. policy to extinguish Indian title, remove them west of the Mississippi and "... guarantee to them by the United States of their exclusive possession of that country forever, exempt from all intrusions by white men ... ,"[33] no effective law existed to keep settlers from continuing to surround Indian nations. The Indian Territory to which so many tribes were removed was eventually invaded as well. Originally comprising most of present-day Oklahoma, Kansas and Nebraska, the Kansas-Nebraska Act of 1854 removed these two territories from the Indians and opened the way for their admission as states of the union. Though many Indian nations retained reservations in these and other states, their ability to do so and retain their government relied largely on the size and desirability of their holdings. If the settlers, or those that profited from them such as the railroads, wanted a particular piece of land badly enough they were almost sure to get it.

Notes

1. As quoted by T.C. McLuhan in *Touch the Earth: A Self-portrait of Indian Existence,* (New York: Promontory Press, 1971), 139. Within 65 years Harkins' forebodings proved prophetic.

2. David E. Wilkins, *American Indian Sovereignty and the U.S. Supreme Court: The Masking of Justice* (Austin: University of Texas, 1997) provides an outstanding series of case studies which trace the development of various "masks" that the Federal Government has used to hide the reality of its policy toward American Indians. Those wishing a more detailed examination of the specific masks

3. *Johnson v. McIntosh,* 8 Wheaton 543 (1823), 572–592.

4. Here Marshall seems to recognize the forced nature of most of the Indian "sales" of land. In fact almost all the land had been purchased, though as we have seen the sale was usually the result of settler intrusion and violence.

5. James Richardson, v 2, p 804.

6. Ibid., v 1, 661.

7. Ibid., v 2, 804–805.

8. Ibid., 938.

9. Ibid., 939.

10. Tim Pickles, *New Orleans 1815: Andrew Jackson Crushes the British,* Osprey Military Campaign Series, vol. 28 ed. David G. Chandler (London: Osprey, 1993), 37. Gives the order of battle of the U.S. forces which included 62 Choctaws.

11. James Richardson, Ibid., 1019–1021.

12. *U.S. Statutes at Large,* 4:411–12.

13. Ibid., 411.
14. Ibid.
15. Ibid.
16. Ibid., 412.
17. Ibid., 1100.
18. Alexis de Tocqueville, *Democracy in America,* ed. by J. P. Maayer, transl. by George Lawrence, (New York: Harper and Row, 1966; Harper-Collins 19th edition), 324–325.
19. TREATY WITH THE CHOCTAW {1820, Oct. 18},7 Stat., 210. Proclamation, Jan. 8, 1821.
20. See Appendix D, number 5.
21. *Cherokee Nation v. Georgia,* 5 Peters 1 (1831), 15–16, 20.
22. Prucha, *Great Father,* 210 provides a short account of the differences among the Justices.
23. *Worcester v. Georgia,* 6 Peters 515 (1832), 559.
24. Felix S. Cohen, *Handbook of Federal Indian Law,* (Washington D.C.: Bureau of Printing, 1943; reprint, Buffalo: William S. Hein, 1988), 90 makes a similar point contrasting this with the notion of plenary power commonly cited today.
25. *Worcester v. Georgia,* Ibid, 551–552.
26. Ibid., 555.
27. Ibid., 561.
28. Ibid., 581–582
29 Ibid., 559–560.
30 Ibid., 561.
31 See Prucha, *Great Father,* 212–213, for a short account of the aftermath of *Worcester v. Georgia.*
32 Ibid., 593.
33 2nd Annual Message, December 3rd 1838, from Richardson, vol. 3, p. 1715.

CHAPTER 4
Decimation and War

> *It matters little where we pass the remnants of our days. They will not be many. The Indians' night promises to be dark. Not a single star of hope hovers above the horizon. Sad-voiced winds moan in the distance. Grim fate seems to be on the Red Man's trail, and wherever he goes he will hear the approaching footsteps of his fell destroyer and prepare stolidly to meet his doom, as does the wounded doe that hears the approaching footsteps of the hunter.*
>
> —Chief Seattle[1]

The spread of settlers and resultant Indian removal caused the deaths of thousands. The 1849 discovery of gold in California brought an influx of settlers and miners who wantonly killed the Indians there. According to Thornton, "Primarily because of the killings, the California Indian population—which some scholars say once had been at least 310,000, perhaps over 700,000—decreased almost two-thirds in little more than a single decade: from 100,000 in 1849 to 35,000 in 1860."[2] Elsewhere, settler violence was prevalent though seldom at the same level as California. Tribes that removed to escape the violence or extension of state authority fared little better. The Choctaws lost about fifteen percent of their population during removal, a comparatively small loss due to their "voluntary" early removal. The Creeks and Seminoles lost about fifty percent of their population, though the latter was mainly from the war that was required to force them to remove. The Cherokees lost about one-third of their population on what came to be known as "The Trail of Tears." Overall Indian population in the U.S. went from 600,000 in 1800 to 250,000 in 1900, while the number of non-Indians went from 5 million to over 75 million in the same period, largely through immigration.[3] Though European diseases took many Indian lives, their spread had started as early as the 16th century. Most Indians of the 19th century should have been almost as resistant as the Europeans. Even for those that weren't as resistant, the hardships brought on by U.S. expansion would have been a factor. Though some of the deaths are related to intertribal warfare, much of this was the result of tribes being forced together as a result of removal. Ultimately, the spread of U.S. settlers must be seen as the primary cause for this decimation.

Despite such problems, many of the Indian nations were doing well in their new homes. In his First Annual Message on December 8th, 1857, President James Buchanan provided clear U.S. recognition of the "civilization" of the Five Tribes.

> The tribes of Cherokees, Choctaws, Chickasaws, and Creeks settled in the Territory set apart for them west of Arkansas are rapidly advancing in education and in all the arts of civilization and self-government and we may indulge the agreeable anticipation that at no very distant day they will be incorporated into the Union as one of the sovereign States.[4]

The U.S. Civil War intervened before this could happen.

Most of the Indian nations were bystanders in the U.S. Civil War, often happy to see the country that had persecuted them dissolve in conflict. The Five Tribes however all signed treaties with the Confederacy, though this brought about a civil war in some. The Creeks and Cherokees in particular had large factions that refused to violate their treaties with the United States. The same sentiment was present in varying degrees in all the Indian nations, though their cavalier treatment at the hands of the United States and the fact that it appeared they had been deserted by the U.S. at the beginning of the war served to break down this resistance. Among the many reasons for the actions of the Five Tribes, it is clear that national sovereignty was an issue. The Choctaws made this quite explicit,

> ... George Hudson, principal chief of the Choctaw Nation, acting in accordance with the will of the National Council, which had met four days before, publicly declared the Choctaw Nation was "free and *independent.*"[5]

Decimation and War 55

The Osages, Senecas, Shawnees and Quapaws also signed treaties with the Confederates, though not on as favorable terms as the Five Tribes.

> Especially notable was the fact that under these treaties a Choctaw-Chickasaw, a Creek-Seminole, and a Cherokee delegate sat in the Confederate Congress throughout the war—a prospect held out to the Indians ever since the Delaware treaty in 1778, but never implemented by the United States.[6]

Outside Indian Territory there was a great deal of turmoil. As Debo describes it,

> There was no consistent pattern. As the military forces were withdrawn for fighting the great battles in the East, the Indians in some places had a breathing space; in others they seized the opportunity of going on the war path; in still others they were the victims of local Indian-haters . . .[7]

The Santee-Sioux (Dakota) in particular, began one of the most bloody uprisings in history. Angered by settler incursion, delay in treaty-guaranteed annuity payments and other grievances they staged raids that killed over 800 settlers.[8] This level of violence fueled the hatreds of settlers in all parts of the country, who had everything to gain and little to lose from war with local Indians. The prime example of this was in Colorado.

> Governor John Evans, rebuffed in efforts to persuade the Cheyennes and Arapahos to exchange their hunting grounds for a reservation, sensed that what could not be gained by diplomacy might fall as a prize of war . . .[9]

The war was pursued despite the fact that most of the Indians sued for peace immediately. Black Kettle and his band had met with Governor Evans and Colonel Chivington, head of the territory's military, to arrange peace. They also sought protection as prisoners of war at a nearby fort. A month later, after raising additional troops for the purpose, Chivington and his territorial troops attacked Black Kettle's band. They killed hundreds, primarily women and children, mutilating their corpses. The attack was carried out while an American flag and a white flag flew over the Cheyenne camp. On their triumphant return to Denver, the territorial troops proudly displayed Indian scalps at a local theater.[10] This outrage resulted in open war with the Cheyenne, Arapaho and Sioux nations and caused tension among all the tribes.

The Sand Creek Massacre also caused a stir of revulsion among many whites, particularly those in the east near the seat of Federal power. With the end of the Civil War and the election of a new president, the Sand Creek Massacre helped set the stage for a change in Federal Indian policy.

> A week before his inauguration in 1869, President-elect Grant told a newspaper reporter that the new administration planned a fresh and fair Indian policy. "All Indians disposed to peace will find the new policy a peace policy," said Grant. For Indians undisposed to peace, he added a caveat drowned in the public acclaim for the Peace Policy, there would be "a sharp and severe war policy." On their reservations the Indians would be educated, Christianized, taught to support themselves by farming, given rations, clothing, and other goods to ease the transition. There too they would be safe from the Army. But if any felt the pull of old habits and strayed off the reservation, they could expect to be treated as hostiles.[11]

Most of the actual administration of Indians on reservations was turned over to religious groups. Grant explains his reasons for turning to religious groups in his First Annual Message of December 6th, 1869,

> From the foundation of the Government to the present the management of the original inhabitants of this continent—the Indians—has been a subject of embarrassment and expense, and has been attended with continuous robberies, murders, and wars. From my own experience upon the frontiers and in Indian countries, I do not hold either legislation or the conduct of the whites who come most in contact with the Indian blameless for these hostilities. The past, however, can not be undone, and the question must be met as we now find it. I have attempted a new policy toward these wards of the nation (they can not be regarded in any other light than as wards), with fair results so far as tried, and which I hope will be attended ultimately with great success. The Society of Friends is well known as having succeeded in living in peace with the Indians in the early settlement of Pennsylvania, while their white neighbors of other sects in

other sections were constantly embroiled. They are also known for their opposition to all strife, violence, and war, and are generally noted for their strict integrity and fair dealings. These considerations induced me to give the management of a few reservations of Indians to them and to throw the burden of the selection of agents upon the society itself . . .[12]

Grant's statement that the Society of Friends was noted for its "strict integrity" is a particularly pointed remark. Just the year before, the Indian Peace Commission had reported that,

The records are abundant to show that agents have pocketed the funds appropriated by the government and driven the Indians to starvation. It cannot be doubted that Indian wars have originated from this cause. The Sioux war, in Minnesota, is supposed to have been produced in this way. For a long time these officers have been selected from partisan ranks, not so much on account of honesty and qualification, as for devotion to party interests and their willingness to apply the money of the Indian to promote the schemes of local politicians.[13]

Grant clearly hoped that the religious guardians of his new peace policy would end the history of corruption in the Indian Office.

Religious leadership was central to the peace policy. As Prucha put it, "The peace policy might just as properly have been labeled the religious policy."[14] Reservation Indians, definitely now in the status of wards, were to be given to the Christians — eventually divided up by sect among various Christian groups. This alliance of church and state would continue as an important element of Indian policy into this century.

Officers of the army were selected as superintendents and Indian agents not on the reservations. These officers, Christian and Army, would be working speedily within the old reservation system, to avert tragedy. As President Grant put it,

The building of railroads, and the access thereby given to all the agricultural and mineral regions of the country, is rapidly bringing civilized settlements into contact with all the tribes of Indians. No matter what ought to be the relations between such settlements and the aborigines, the fact is they do not harmonize well, and one or the other has to give way in the end. A system which looks to the extinction of a race is too horrible for a nation to adopt without entailing upon itself the wrath of all Christendom and engendering in the citizen a disregard for human life and the rights of others, dangerous to society. I see no substitute for such a system, except in placing all the Indians on large reservations, as rapidly as it can be done, and giving them absolute protection there. As soon as they are fitted for it they should be induced to take their lands in severalty and to set up Territorial governments for their own protection.[15]

Emergent elements of this policy included the allotment of lands in severalty and the idea of the Natives banding together in Territorial governments for their own "protection." The severalty issue would slowly develop into the allotment policy that would typify the end of the nineteenth century. Indian land ownership had always been "in common." But private ownership was a bulwark of the U.S. system. In the views of non-Indian policymakers, the private ownership of land was clearly better, offering incentives to work that did not exist in the communal system of the Indians. Grant's musings about Indian territorial governments, just like prior and subsequent musings about Indian states, never came to pass. His linking of such territorial governments to their protection, seems to indicate that only U.S. citizens could expect real protection against the depredations of other U.S. citizens, though of course Grant could not state this openly. Treaties still supposedly guaranteed protection for the remaining Indians.

The military side of the peace policy was in the hands of William Tecumseh Sherman and Phillip Henry Sheridan who "...believed in total war against the entire enemy population..."[16] Their field commanders were former Civil War generals like George A. Custer, now returned to their permanent ranks of colonel or lower. They were "spoiling for action—of the kind that would bring fame and permanent promotion to general."[17] Sherman himself had said in 1866, "God only knows when, and I do not see how, we can make a decent excuse for an Indian war."[18]

The peace policy was an effective carrot-and-stick formulation that did not change the general thrust of dispossession and concentration, it merely refined it. Outraged whites were mollified by the seeming change as well as some clear benefits under the peace policy. The new Indian agents and functionaries were churchmen who were usually not as corrupt as their predecessors. Goods and monies appropriated for Indian nations reached their intended destinations for a time, until corruption again won out.[19] The Federal

Army's direct hand in the dispossession meant that most of the killing of Indians would usually take place in open warfare rather than in brutal murders and massacres that had characterized the actions of civilians and the territorial militias. Unfortunately, the no-compromise nature of the peace policy meant that the warfare would be almost constant until the end of the 1880's.

As the peace policy was implemented, at least some tribes were considered well advanced in civilization by U.S. officials. In the 1869 case *United States v. Lucero*,[20] Pueblo Indians were lauded above even American citizens.

> This court has known the conduct and habits of these Indians for eighteen or twenty years, and we say, without fear of successful contradiction, that you may pick out one thousand of the best Americans in New Mexico, and one thousand of the best Mexicans in New Mexico, and one thousand of the worst Pueblo Indians, and there will be found less, vastly less, murder, robbery, theft, or other crimes among the thousand worst Pueblos than among the thousand best Mexicans or Americans in New Mexico.[21]

Using this reasoning the court forbade interference with the Pueblo government, reasoning which the U.S. Supreme Court would uphold in the 1876 case *United States v. Joseph*.[22] Yet, less than forty years later the Supreme Court would reverse itself in *United States v. Sandoval*.

> The people of the pueblos, although sedentary rather than nomadic in their inclinations, and disposed to peace and industry, are nevertheless Indians in race, customs, and domestic government. Always living in separate and isolated communities, adhering to primitive modes of life, largely influenced by superstition and fetishism, and chiefly governed according to the crude customs inherited from their ancestors, they are essentially a simple, uninformed, and inferior people.[23]

Whatever the status of the various Indian nations, the peace policy would see their concentration onto reservations within two decades. The undermanned Federal Army would be aided in its efforts by white hunters and settlers who killed the game and turned the grasslands into farms. With little or no game to hunt, the tribes were forced to accept reservations. This pattern had already served a role in the removal of the eastern tribes. Though these tribes, particularly the Five Tribes, practiced a significant amount of agriculture, their food supply was supplemented by increased hunting in bad-harvest years. Game animals were an absolutely essential backup food supply in a region and era where long-term food storage was problematic.[24]

Tribes dependent on game were even more vulnerable to the effects of white over-hunting. This included most of the Plains tribes, which were dependent on buffalo (the common name for all varieties of the North American Bison).[25] As usual, private profit was the main motive for depriving the Indians; and equally as usual, the Federal Government would not stop the depredation. Enterprising whites had discovered how to tan buffalo hides to produce fine leather. Within a few years the Great Plains stank from the smell of putrefying buffalo carcasses, as hide hunters killed the animals by the millions; skinned them and left the remains to rot. Between 1870 and 1890, as the peace policy worked to force the plains tribes onto reservations, the buffalo population dropped from 14,000,000 to a little over 1,000.[26] When buffalo were wiped out on white land, the hunters moved onto lands reserved for Indian hunting and even onto lands owned by the Indians. Such hunters asked Colonel Dodge what he would do if they moved onto Indian hunting grounds in Texas.

> "Boys," said the Colonel, "if I were a buffalo hunter, I would hunt where the buffalo are."
>
> So much for the protection the Indians could expect in preserving their hunting grounds. Dodge's slightly veiled proposal to the hide men to move across into the Panhandle was a deliberate invitation to trouble with the Indians, and he was not so naïve as not to have known it. However, he was not speaking carelessly and expressing only his own views; Sherman, Sheridan, and other (but not all) Army officers had taken the position that the quickest way to tame the roving Indians and keep them on the reservations would be to hurry up the extermination of the buffalo.[27]

There were many reasons to stop the killing but,

> The army, in fact, was instrumental in preventing any halt to the slaughter. Many Texans had become appalled at what was called an insane butchery of God's creatures, and a bill was in-

troduced in the state legislature to halt all such hunting. This bill was strongly opposed by leather lobbies and ranching interests—for the western cowmen saw the bison as useless and an obstacle—but it would have probably been enacted, had not Sheridan, with Sherman's approval, made a special trip to Austin to address the legislature. Sheridan argued vehemently that to oppose the killing of the buffalo was to oppose the advance of civilization. The alliance of ranchers, eastern leather-makers, soldiers, and Indian-haters won over the politicians. The bill was killed and never resurrected.[28]

The Plains tribes joined the previously "pacified" tribes on reservations as their way of life was destroyed. The peace policy recognized only two types of Indians, the hostile and the pacified; those that had not been forced onto reservations yet and those that had already been forced onto them. Such a clear distinction admitted of little negotiation. When carried to its conclusion all Indian tribes would be subjugated. This attitude spread to all parts of the Federal Government. After 1871 Congress voted to make no more treaties with Indian tribes.[29] The general rationale for this is laid out in Indian Affairs Commissioner Ely S. Parker's annual report of 1869.

> It has become a matter of serious import whether the treaty system in use ought longer to be continued. In my judgment it should not. A treaty involves the idea of a compact between two or more sovereign powers, each possessing sufficient authority and force to compel a compliance with the obligations incurred. The Indian tribes of the United States are not sovereign nations, capable of making treaties, as none of them have an organized government of such inherent strength as would secure a faithful obedience of its people in the observance of compacts of this character. They are held to be wards of the government, and the only title the law concedes to them to the lands they occupy or claim is a mere possessory one. . . . Many good men looking at this matter only from a Christian point of view, will perhaps say that the poor Indian has been greatly wronged and ill treated; that this whole country was once his, of which he has been despoiled . . . but the stern letter of the law admits of no such conclusion . . .[30]

Though Parker seems to recognize the inherent injustice of the position, as many before him, he still asserts that it is the law. The relation of superior to inferior is now clear after having built up over decades. Indians are wards, if only because of the action of the Federal Government. Most ironically, Parker claims that one cannot make a treaty with Indians because their government cannot compel obedience. He seems unaware of the history of treaty breaking engaged in by his own people.

For their part, the courts slowly turn away from Indian sovereignty. McLean cites the commerce clause and the treaties to this end in 1855.

> A question has been suggested whether the Cherokee people should be considered and treated as a foreign state or territory. The fact that they are under the constitution of the Union, and subject to acts of congress regulating trade, is sufficient to answer this suggestion. They are not only within our jurisdiction, but the faith of the nation is pledged for their protection.[31]

In 1870, District Judge Caldwell cites McLean and uses the long history of U.S. arrogation of the right to try cases that involve U.S. citizens in disputes with Indians, to strike down parts of a treaty and explicitly deny Indian sovereignty.

> Ever since the organization of this court it has sat here administering and enforcing the laws of the United States over the Indian country. Indians are taken from that country, brought here for trial, and are tried and punished—in some instances capitally. They are prohibited from trafficking in certain articles.... They are without a single attribute that marks a sovereign and independent people.[32]

Despite such pronouncements, Indian self-governance continued on the reservations. On most reservations, the Christian groups assigned to administer Federal policy did not control the government. They proselytized, educated and tried to push the tribes that were not already doing so into governing themselves along the same lines as the United States, but they seldom dictated. Various Federal laws applied to Indian people, but they were mainly ones that pertained to interaction with non-Indians. The killing of Spotted Tail by Crow Dog would change all that. Spotted Tail was a peaceful Brûlé Sioux chief who had maintained close and friendly relations with the United States. The killing was handled traditionally and the matter was closed from standpoint of the tribe, but whites desired vengeance for the death of their friend.[33] Like *Worcester v. Georgia,* the 1883 case of *ex Parte Crow Dog* was a nominal victory for the Native nation. Because it was an Indian on Indian crime in Indian country, the court ruled that no relevant U.S. law was broken by the killing. However, it explicitly opened the way for such laws.

> ... The pledge to secure to these people, with whom the United States was contracting as a distinct political body, an orderly form of government, by appropriate legislation thereafter to be framed and enacted, necessarily implies, having regard to all the circumstances attending the transaction, that among the arts of civilized life, which it was the very purpose of all these arrangements to introduce and naturalize among them, was the highest of all, self-government, the regulation by themselves of their own domestic affairs, the maintenance of order and peace among their own members by the administration of their own laws and customs. They were nevertheless to be subject to the laws of the United States, not in the sense of citizens, but, as they had always been, as wards subject to a guardian; not as individuals, constituted members of the political community of the United States, with a voice in the selection of representatives and the framing of laws, but as a dependent community who were in a state of pupilage, advancing from the condition of a savage tribe to that of a people who, through the discipline of labor and by education, it was hoped might become a self-supporting and self-governing society.[34]

The U.S. guardian could thus enact laws to cover such actions and it did. The Major Crimes Act[35] of 1885, covered a variety of acts committed by Indians against Indians within Indian country.

This legislation was upheld in *United States v. Kagama* in 1886.

> Following the policy of the European governments in the discovery of America towards the Indians who were found here, the colonies before the Revolution and the States and the United States since, have recognized in the Indians a possessory right to the soil over which they hunted and established occasional villages. But they asserted an ultimate title in the land itself, by which the Indian tribes were forbidden to sell or to transfer it to

other nations or peoples without the consent of this paramount authority. When a tribe wished to dispose of its land, or any part of it, or the State or the United States wished to purchase it, a treaty was the only mode in which it could be done. The United States recognized no right in private persons, or in other nations, to make purchase by treaty or otherwise. With the Indians themselves these relations are equally difficult to define. They were, and always have been, regarded as having a semi-independent position when they preserve their tribal relations; not as States, not as nations, not as possessed of the full attributes of sovereignty, but as a separate people, with the power of regulating their internal and social relations, and thus far not brought under the laws of the Union or of the State within whose limits they resided. . . .

It seems to us that this [extension of U.S. law into Indian country] is within the competency of Congress. These Indian tribes are the wards of the nation. They are communities *dependent* on the United States. Dependent largely for their daily food. Dependent for their political rights. They owe no allegiance to the States, and receive from them no protection. Because of local ill feeling, the people of the States are often their deadliest enemies. From their very weakness and helplessness, so largely due to the course of dealing of the Federal Government with them and the treaties in which it has been promised, there arises a duty of protection, and with it the power. This has always been recognized by the Executive and by Congress, and by this court, whenever the question has arisen. . . .

The power of the General Government over these remnants of a race once powerful, now weak and diminished in numbers, is necessary to their protection, as well as to the safety of those among whom they dwell. It must exist in that government, because it never has existed anywhere else, because the theatre of its exercise is within the geographical limits of the United States, because it has never been denied, and because it alone can enforce its laws over all the tribes.[36]

Miller's decision rests on two main points, that the doctrine of discovery assumes a certain paramountcy which necessarily diminished Indian sovereignty from the beginning and that the course of events had forced the Indian nations into dependent roles that required guardianship. The role of guardianship presumes the power and the Federal Government had always been supreme under the doctrine of discovery anyway, so they are the ones wielding the power.

The presumption of power over Indians within their reservation was a watershed. Relations between the U.S. and Indian nations had progressed from a relationship between sovereigns to a relationship between a stronger sovereign and a weaker one over whom the former exercised protection, and now to a relationship between a sovereign and a people over whom they exercised complete authority as ward. Indian nations had not voluntarily ended their governments and asked to be amalgamated with the United States. Far from it, they had resisted at every step. Now they would be forced to understand the benefits of the American form of democratic government. The Federal Government would dictate internal policies to the Indian nations, supposedly for their benefit. The greatest benefit would be absorption into the United States, but the Indian practice of common ownership of land stood in the way.

Notes

1. As quoted by W.C. Vanderwerth in *Indian Oratory: Famous Speeches By Noted Chieftains,* The Civilization of the American Indian Series, volume 110, (Norman and London: University of Oklahoma, 1971), 120.

2. Russell Thornton, *American Indian Holocaust and Survival: A Population History Since 1492,* (Norman and London: University of Oklahoma, 1987), 109.

3. Ibid.,114–115, 118, 133 either directly provides mortality and population figures, or provides information from which they are calculated.

4. James Richardson, vol. 4, p. 2991.

5. Annie Heloise Abel, *The American Indian as Slaveholder and Secessionist,* (Cleveland: Arthur H. Clark, 1915; reprint, Lincoln and London: University of Nebraska, 1992), 156. This work also provides a detailed examination of other factors at work within the tribes.

6. Angie Debo, *A History of the Indians of the United States,* The Civilization of the American Indian Series vol. 106, (Norman and London: University of Oklahoma, 1970), 172.

7. Ibid., 184.

8. For an account of this conflict see Robert M. Utley and Wolcombe E. Washburn, *Indian Wars,* (Boston: Houghton Mifflin, 1977), 202–204. This book is also a very good overall history of the Indian wars in the U.S.

9. Ibid., 206.

10. See Ibid., 207., Prucha, *Great Father*, 459 and Stan Hoig, *The Sand Creek Massacre*, (Norman: University of Oklahoma, 1961).

11. Utley and Wolcombe, 226–227.

12. James Richardson, Ibid., vol. 6, 3992–3.

13. *House Executive Document* no. 97, 40th Cong., 2nd sess., serial 1337. As reproduced in Prucha, *Documents of U.S. Indian Policy*, 108.

14. Prucha, *Great Father*, 482.

15. Ibid.

16. Utley and Wolcombe, 210.

17. Ibid., 211.

18. As quoted by Debo, 215.

19. See Prucha, *Great Father*, 525 for an account of the return to corruption.

20. 1 N.M. 422.

21. 1 N.M 441.

22. *United States v. Joseph*, 94 U.S. 614 (1876), 617.

23. *United States v. Sandoval*, 231 U.S. 28 (1913), 39.

24. Richard White, *The Roots of Dependency: Subsistence, Environment and Social Change Among the Choctaws, Pawnees, and Navajos*, (Lincoln and London: University of Nebraska, 1983), 29–33. Provides an account of the secondary subsistence pattern of Choctaws as well as the settler role in destroying this food supply.

25. Interestingly, it was the introduction of horses and guns by Europeans that caused these tribes to become so dependent on the buffalo.

26. Thornton, Table 3-1 on page 52 gives buffalo population figures.

27. Ralph K. Andrist, *The Long Death: The Last Days of the Plains Indian*, (New York: Collier Books, 1969; New Collier Books, 1993), 183.

28. T.R. Fehrenbach, *Comanches: The Destruction of a People*, (New York: Alfred A. Knopf, 1974; New York: Da Capo, 1994), 525.

29. The end of treaty making came in an appropriations bill rider, stating that tribes were no longer the sort of entities that the U.S. could contract with by treaty. It did, however, point out that prior treaties were binding. *U.S. Statutes at Large*, 16:566.

30. Prucha, *Documents of U.S. Indian Policy*, 134–135.

31. *Mackey v. Coxe*, 18 How. 100 (1855).

32. *United States v. Tobacco*, 28 Fed. Cas., 195 (1870), 196–197.

33. Vine Deloria, Jr. and Clifford Lytle, *American Indians American Justice*, (Austin: University of Texas, 1983), 168–169 gives a somewhat more detailed account.

34. *Ex Parte Crow Dog*, 109 U.S. 556 (1883), 568–569.

35. *U.S. Statutes at Large*, 23:385.

36. *United States v. Kagama*, 118 U.S. 375 (1886), 381–385.

CHAPTER 5
Allotment to the Present

> *Under the old Cherokee regime I spent the early days of my life on the farm up here of 300 acres, and arranged to be comfortable in my old age . . .*
>
> *. . . I have 60 acres of land left to me; the balance is all gone.*
>
> *What am I to do? I have a piece of property that doesn't support me, and is not worth a cent to me, under the same inexorable, cruel provisions of the Curtis law that swept away our treaties, our system of nationality, our every existence, and wrested out of our possession our vast country . . .*
>
> —*Dewitt Clinton Duncan, Cherokee*[1]

Despite the fact that common ownership seemed to work for most Indian people of the time, it was in direct opposition to the free-market, private enterprise, profit motivated American system. Senator Henry Dawes sought to justify allotment by speaking of his recent examination trip among the Cherokees:

> There was not a pauper in that nation, and the nation did not owe a dollar. It built its own capitol, in which we had this examination, and it built its schools and its hospitals. Yet the defect of the system was apparent. They have gone as far as they can go, because they own their land in common. It is Henry Georges's system, and under that there is no enterprise to make your home any better than that of your neighbors. There is no selfishness, which is at the bottom of civilization. Till this people will consent to give up their lands, and divide them among their own citizens so that each can own the land he cultivates, they will not make much more progress.[2]

Amazingly, just a year later, the Board of Indian Commissioners would use a contradiction of this argument as a further argument for allotment.

> At present the rich Indians who cultivate tribal lands pay no rent to the poorer and more unfortunate of their race, although they are equal owners of the soil. The rich men have too large homesteads and control many times more than their share of land. . . . Already the rich and choice lands are appropriated by those most enterprising and self seeking.[3]

It didn't matter whether their enterprise was retarded by common ownership of land, or they had managed to use the system to promote entrepreneurial free enterprise. Contradictory as the arguments were, common ownership of land had to go.

The Board also reiterated the theme of the "absurdity" of governments within governments to justify the forced absorption of the tribes.

> While I greatly prefer that these people should voluntarily change their form of government, yet it is perfectly plain to my mind that the treaties never contemplated the un-American and absurd idea of a separate nationality in our midst . . . These Indians have no right to obstruct civilization and commerce and set up an exclusive claim to self-government, establishing a government within a government . . . I repeat, to maintain any such view is to acknowledge a foreign sovereignty, with the right of eminent domain, upon American soil—a theory utterly repugnant to the spirit and genius of our laws and wholly unwarranted by the Constitution of the United States.[4]

Some self-proclaimed "friends of the Indians" not only supported allotment, but seemed to say that it might be best for the Indians to *lose* their property in the process. As Merrill Gates said, "We have found it necessary, as one of the first steps in developing a stronger personality in the Indian, to make him responsible for property. Even if he learns its value only by losing it, and going without it until he works for more, the educational process has begun."[5]

Though many whites supported allotment and argued for it in various ways, their motives were occasionally called into question. The minority report of the House Indian Affairs Commission concerning an early version of the allotment bill was quite clear on the motives.

> The real aim of this bill is to get at the Indian lands and open them up for settlement. The provisions for the apparent benefit of the Indian are but the pretext to get at his lands and occupy them.... If this were done in the name of greed it would be bad enough; but to do it in the name of humanity, and under the cloak of an ardent desire to promote the Indian's welfare by making him like ourselves, whether he will or not, is infinitely worse.[6]

These words, seemingly prophetic, were more nearly hindsight. History to this time had certainly shown a greed for Indian land, but more importantly Native Americans had already been deprived of their lands under allotment. Tribal remnants had received allotments going back at least to the 1830's, and their experiences had often been horrific. In 1888 Grover Cleveland wrote to Congress about one of these cases. Of more than 200 New York Indians with allotments in Kansas, he said,

> From death and the hostility of the settlers, who were drawn in that direction by the fertility of the soil and other advantages, all of the Indians gradually relinquished their selections, until of the Indians who had removed thither from the State of New York only thirty-two remained in 1860....
>
> The files of the Indian Office show abundant proof that they did not voluntarily relinquish their occupation.
>
> The proof thus referred to is indeed abundant, and is found in official reports and affidavits made as late as the year 1859. By these it appears that during that year, in repeated instances, Indian men and widows of deceased Indians were driven from their homes by the threats of armed men; that in one case at least the habitation of an Indian woman was burned, and that the kind of outrages were resorted to which too often follow the cupidity of whites and the possession of fertile lands by defenseless and unprotected Indians....
>
> [quoting an Indian agent] These Indians have been driven off their land and claims upon the New York tract by the whites, and they are now very much scattered and many of them are very destitute.
>
> It was found in 1860 that of all the Indians who had prior to that date selected and occupied part of these lands but thirty-two remained, and it seems to have been deemed but justice to them to confirm their selections by some kind of governmental

> grant or declaration, though it does not appear that any of them had been able to maintain actual possession of all their selected lands against white intrusion....
>
> In 1861 and 1862 mention was made by the agents of the destitute condition of these Indians and of their being deprived of their lands, and in these years petitions were presented in their behalf asking that justice be done them on account of the failure of the Government to provide them with homes.
>
> In the meantime, and in December, 1860, the remainder of the reserve not allotted to the thirty-two survivors was thrown open to settlement by Executive proclamation. Of course this was followed by increased conflict between the settlers and the Indians. It is presumed that it became dangerous for those to whom lands had been allotted to attempt to gain possession of them. On the 4th day of December, 1865, Agent Snow returned twenty-seven of the certificates of allotment which had not been delivered, and wrote as follows to the Indian Bureau:
>
> A few of these Indians were at one time put in possession of their lands. They were driven off by the whites; one Indian was killed, others wounded, and their houses burned. White men at this time have possession of these lands, and have valuable improvements on them. The Indians are deterred even asking for possession. I would earnestly ask, as agent for these wronged and destitute people, that some measure be adopted by the Government to give these Indians their rights....
>
> ... There is great necessity that some relief should be afforded to them by legislation of Congress, authorizing the issue of patents to the allottees or giving them power to sell and convey.
>
> In this way they will be enabled to realize something from the land, and the occupants can secure titles for their homes....
>
> The occupancy upon these lands of the settlers seeking relief, and of their grantors, is based upon wrong, violence, and oppression. A continuation of the wrongful exclusion of these Indians from their lands should not inure to the benefit of the wrongdoers.[7]

It is interesting to note that this case had been documented for more than 28 years by the time Grover Cleveland asked for action. It might never have been addressed had it not been for the passage of the General Allotment Act. To have Indians destitute from past allotments on hand when the remaining Indians were to be accorded the same treatment was all too embarrassing. As it was, this case and others provide significant foreshadowing of the events that would occur under the General Allotment Act.

The General Allotment Act[8] or "Dawes Act" was passed in 1887, only two years after Congress extended its criminal jurisdiction over Indian country. This act authorized the breakup of reservations into individually owned plots of land. Indians accepting allotments and adopting "the habits of civilized life" would automatically be made citizens of the United States. The end result was supposed to be the dissolution of the tribes. Though the allotments were fairly large, even when parceled out to every tribal member it did not take all the holdings of the tribe to furnish the plots. This meant that there was a surplus. As with the 1860 allotment, it was a surplus that would be given to whites.

Several tribes, most notably the Five Tribes, were exempted from the General Allotment Act for a variety of reasons. They were politically astute and able to lobby on their own behalf; they had relatively successful governments with constitutions; they had prosperous citizens; and some, like the Choctaw, had treaties that seemed to preclude the act.[9] They were under constant pressure to accept allotment, but consistently refused. Though the refusal was partially based on the importance of common ownership of land, it was as much a matter of citizenship. An illustration of this is the Choctaw reaction to the Oklahoma Organic Act of 1890[10] which, among other things, allowed Indians in Indian Territory to apply for U.S. citizenship without forfeiting tribal rights.

> The Choctaws were greatly aroused over this attempt to undermine their government, and strong efforts were made to prevent their citizens from taking the oath of allegiance to the United States. When the Council met, a law was passed disqualifying such apostates from voting, holding office, or serving on the jury. The United States had expected that large numbers would apply for citizenship, but almost the only applications came from a few who had violated Choctaw law and wished to escape the jurisdiction of the tribal courts.[11]

The main effect of the Oklahoma Organic Act was to further whittle down the Indian Territory. The Territory of Oklahoma was created out of that portion of Indian Territory not owned by the Five Tribes. Thus by the end of 1890, Indian Territory had been reduced to the holdings of the Five Tribes. The Five Tribes steadfastly maintained their treaty rights in the face of growing pressure for allotment. By 1894, the Dawes Commission was using the oldest argument for the allotment of Five Tribes land.

> The resources of the Territory itself have been developed to such a degree and are of such immense and tempting value that they are attracting to it an irresistible pressure from enterprising citizens. The executory conditions contained in the treaties have become impossible of execution. It is no longer possible for the United States to keep its citizens out of Indian Territory.[12]

Allotment was forced on the Five Tribes by the Curtis Act of 1898.[13] Possibly fearing the strength and resilience of the Five Tribes governments, the U.S. government undertook specific legislation to abolish them. "Negotiations" arrived at a target date of March 4th, 1906 for the abolition of tribal government, though in 1910 Indian Affairs Commissioner Leupp described the process more correctly,

> . . . [B]y successive acts of Congress the Five Civilized Tribes were shorn of their governmental functions; their courts were abolished and the United States Courts established; their chief executive officers were made subject to removal by the President, who was authorized to fill by appointment the vacancies thus created; provision was made for the supersession of their tribal schools by a public school system maintained by general taxation; their tribal taxes were abolished; the sale of their public buildings and lands was ordered; their legislatures were forbidden to remain in session more than thirty days in any one year; and every legislative act, ordinance and resolution was declared invalid unless it received the approval of the President. The only present shadow or fiction of the survival of the tribes as tribes is their grudging recognition till all their property or proceeds thereof, can be distributed among individual members.[14]

Despite the U.S. government's efforts, the Five Tribes' governments continued in existence because of the protracted length of the allotment process. It was much easier to deal with the Indians through their own governmental mechanisms. Besides, there was little risk. If anything important came up the U.S. government could always force the tribal government to act as a rubber-stamp, or impose a veto.

As allotment proceeded, there was agitation to unite Oklahoma Territory and Indian Territory to form one state. In 1905, with abolition of their governments and amalgamation into a non-Indian state imminent, representatives of the Five Tribes attempted to form a separate state of the union to maintain some element of self-government. Local conventions were held to elect delegates to a constitutional convention. The constitution was drafted, ratified and sent to the U.S. Congress.

> The whole movement was a most expressive demonstration of the political vitality that still existed in the Indian citizenship. The white residents had been invited to participate, but they took little interest, and the press and public sentiment seemed to be generally hostile. The account of any of the local conventions with its tribal leaders in attendance, its debates in English and the local Indian language, and its smoothly running parliamentary procedure is strongly reminiscent of the great days of tribal politics . . .[15]

Despite historical recognition of their fitness for statehood, the U.S. Congress did not consider the Five Tribes' request. Instead, in 1906, the Enabling Act[16] united the territories and opened the way for Oklahoma's statehood, which finally occurred on November 16th, 1907. President Theodore Roosevelt, welcoming Oklahoma into the union in his 7th Annual Message of December 3rd 1907 sought to reassure the Indian people, "Oklahoma has become a State, standing on a full equality with her elder sisters, and her future is assured by her great natural resources. The duty of the National Government to guard the personal and property rights of the Indians within her borders remains of course unchanged."[17]

Despite Roosevelt's assurances the Indian people were devastated by allotment, particularly in the new state of Oklahoma. Whole books have been devoted to the topic, so a lengthy exposition of its effects are unnecessary for the present work. The first and one of the best books on allotment is Angie Debo's *And Still the Waters Run*.[18] As described there and elsewhere, allotment was a lengthy process that began with the compilation of a census roll generally referred to as the "final roll" for that tribe. Apocalyptic as that sounded, it is not surprising that many people resisted inclusion on the roll. To accept allotment was to accept the final repudiation of solemn treaties; to accept the loss of your nation. In the end virtually all accepted allotment because it was the only way to keep any land. But the land they retained would not be theirs for long. Allotment was implemented by appointed officials who, almost to a man, held stock in land speculation companies. Dozens of schemes were used by whites to gain control first of "surplus" land and then of the land and money of individual Indians. Rennard Strickland provided a short summary of such schemes.

> We could not possibly examine in detail the entire process of the seizure. A few of the more common devices were:
>
> 1. Fraudulent deeds, approved by courts of law, signed by other than the owner of the land;
> 2. Purchase prices far below market or actual appraised value of the land, again approved by courts of law;
> 3. Payments of bribes for court approval of fraudulent land sales;
> 4. Excessive administration and guardianship fees;
> 5. Embezzlement of Indian money and personal expenditure of trust funds for the benefit of the trustee;
> 6. False heirship claims or destruction of Indian wills; and
> 7. Gifts to charities or individual citizens of Indian assets without knowledge or approval of the Indian.[19]

The worst of the schemes even involved murder. As John Wunder explained, "Guardians appointed for Indian minors grossly abused their trust, some even to the extent of murdering their wards. Indians who made out wills leaving their allotments to non-Indians suddenly and mysteriously died."[20]

During the decades of allotment first one then another faction would prevail in the U.S. Congress. Legislation swung the spectrum from protecting Indian property to facilitating its acquisition by whites. Even the protective legislation wasn't of much help. White entrepreneurs were often able to take advantage of it.

Perhaps the clearest statement of the practical effect of allotment is an oft-quoted statistic produced by the U.S. Government when debating an end to allotment. According to the Government, Indian landholdings shrank from 138,000,000 acres before allotment to only 48,000,000 when allotment was ended.[21] Bad as that sounded, the U.S. Government admitted that it was worse. The statistics were

> ... misleading for of the remaining 48,000,000 acres, more than 20,000 acres are contained within areas which for special rea-

sons have been exempted from the allotment law; whereas the land loss is chargeable exclusively against the allotment system.

Furthermore, that part of the allotted land which has been lost is the most valuable part. Of the residual lands, taking all the Indian-owned lands into account, nearly one half, or nearly 20,000,000 acres, are desert or semidesert . . .

. . . For about 100,000 Indians the divestment has been absolute. They are totally landless as a result of allotment.

. . . Through the allotment system, more than 80 percent of the land value belonging to all the Indians in 1887 has been taken away from them; more than 85 percent of the land value of allotted Indians has been taken away.[22]

In Oklahoma, the situation was perhaps the worst. Oklahoma Indians land holdings dropped from 20 million acres to 3 million acres under allotment.[23] As past experience had indicated and the minority opinion of Congress had prophesied, allotment turned out to be little more than a way of taking land away from the Indians.[24]

Many Indian nations went to court for relief from allotment. The most important decision resulting from these cases is the 1903 Supreme Court decision in *Lone Wolf v. Hitchcock*.[25] The Kiowa's had attempted to protect their lands in the 1867 Treaty of Medicine Lodge.[26] Article 12 of that treaty read,

No treaty for the cession of any portion or part of the reservation herein described, which may be held in common, shall be of any validity or force as against the said Indians, unless executed and signed by at least three-fourths of all the adult male Indians occupying the same, and no cession by the tribe shall be understood or construed in such manner as to deprive, without his consent, any individual member of the tribe of his rights to any tract of land selected by him as provided in Article 3 of this treaty.

Since the requisite number of signatures had not been gathered, the Kiowas felt that allotment could not proceed in the way the U.S. government had imposed.

Justice White's majority opinion in the case made it clear that congressional plenary power included the breaking of treaties. The court also made it clear that they would not even exercise judicial review over such an exercise of power.[27]

> The provisions in article 12 of the Medicine Lodge treaty of 1867 . . . cannot be adjudged to materially limit and qualify the controlling authority of Congress in respect to the care and protection of the Indians and to deprive Congress, in a possible emergency, when the necessity might be urgent for a partition and disposal of the tribal lands, of all power to act. . . . Congress has always exercised plenary authority over the tribal relations of the Indians and the power has always been deemed a political one not subject to be controlled by the courts.
>
> In view of the legislative power possessed by Congress over treaties with the Indians . . . the action of Congress is conclusive upon the courts.
>
> The power exists to abrogate the provisions of an Indian treaty, though presumably such power will be exercised only when circumstances arise which will not only justify the government in disregarding the stipulations of the treaty, but may demand, in the interest of the country and the Indians themselves, that it should be so. . . .
>
> . . . If injury was occasioned, which we do not wish to be understood as implying, by the use made by Congress of its power, relief must be sought by an appeal to that body for redress and not to the courts.[28]

Despite the efforts of the Indian nations, the new state Oklahoma[29] had arisen to encompass them. It appeared political amalgamation was a fact. Indians with allotments would become citizens of the U.S. Disregarding a government report[30] stating that Indians did not want citizenship, Congress would force citizenship on the remaining Indians with the Citizenship Act[31] of 1924. This act was a serious departure for the Congress. Prior to this the Indian's allegiance[32] had been a key issue. The U.S. government recognized that their allegiance was to their tribal governments and were thus not made citizens by the accident of having been born within the territorial limits of the U.S.

> Indians born within the territorial limits of the United States, members of, and owing immediate allegiance to, one of the Indian tribes, (an alien though dependent power,) although in a geographical sense born in the United States, are no more "born in the United States and subject to the jurisdiction thereof," within the meaning of the first section of the fourteenth amendment, than the children of subjects of any foreign government born

within the domain of that government, or the children born within the United States, of ambassadors or other public ministers of foreign nations.[33]

Earlier acts, like the General Allotment Act, had required either the passive acceptance of an allotment, which presumably severed tribal ties, or a positive act on the part of the Indian to sever tribal ties,

> ... And every Indian born within the territorial limits of the United States to whom allotments shall have been made under provision of this act, or under any law or treaty, and every Indian born within the territorial limits of the United States who has voluntarily taken up, within said limits, his residence separate and apart from any tribe of Indians therein, and has adopted civilized life is hereby declared to be a citizen of the United States ...[34]

The Indian Citizenship Act required neither positive action nor passivity on the part of the individual, it imposed citizenship regardless. It did not require the taking of an oath of allegiance like naturalization required; Indians were unlikely to freely change allegiance. Thus Native Americans came to hold a unique position in U.S. society, recognized as having dual allegiance — one of which is imposed by the U.S. government.[35]

Passage of the act was comparatively easy. It appeared to grant a boon to Indians, while actually changing their status very little. In their tribal relations they were still under the guardianship of the government and it was fairly easy to deny them the franchise. In some states Native Americans were effectively denied the vote until the 1950's. Thus for the whites there was little to lose and everything to gain. Citizenship seemed to mean a step toward assimilation; removal of restrictions on alienation of Indian property; and taxation. In return, it granted little but unwanted citizenship, though citizenship would make it easier to militate for individual rights.[36]

To facilitate the move to citizenship under allotment, the U.S. government established a series of schools meant to replace the church-run schools of the peace policy.[37] BIA schools provided most of the education for Indian children through the 1920's and a significant amount through World War II. Their numbers declined somewhat in 1934 and steadily declined after World War II, though some remain to this day. There was a slow evolution of the schools, but until the 1960's they taught basic academic and job skills in the English language within a patriotic, Christian framework, stressing individuality and self-reliance. Punishment was often brutal[38] and was aimed at stamping-out the child's "Indianness," particularly their native language. Many of the schools were boarding schools that removed the children from their parents. Initially this was done forcibly, but in the mid 1890's this was forbidden.[39] Partly to teach skills, but mainly as a cost-cutting measure, almost all labor for the maintenance and operation of the schools was supplied by the children. In 1928, the U.S. government sponsored Meriam report stated that the nature of this labor would ". . . constitute a violation of the child labor laws in most states."[40] The amount of work done by the children declined after this, though they still did much of the work. The older generation of Native Americans alive today contains many boarding school alumni who recount the hard work, harsh discipline and loss of native language that characterized the boarding schools.

Despite allotment, citizenship and schooling, Indian people still did not fit in U.S. society. The main effect of the policies had been to take Indian land and attempt to deprive them of their culture. By the 1930's this process was clearly a failure. In a nation wracked by depression, Indian people were the worst-off of all. Reformers sought to fix the problem with the Wheeler-Howard Act of 1934, also known as the Indian Reorganization Act.[41] Though Oklahoma Indians were initially exempted from the more important provisions of the act, they were finally included by the Oklahoma Indian Welfare Act of 1936.[42]

In urging passage of the Wheeler-Howard Act, President Roosevelt made clear some of its reasoning and aims.

> The Wheeler-Howard Bill embodies the basic and broad principles of the Administration for a new standard of dealing between the Federal Government and its Indian wards.
> It is, in the main, a measure of justice that is long overdue. We can and should, without further delay, extend to the Indian the fundamental rights of political liberty and local self-government and the opportunities of education and economic assistance that they require in order to attain a wholesome American life. This is but the obligation of honor of a powerful Nation toward a people living among us and dependent upon our protection.

> Certainly the continuance of autocratic rule, by a Federal Department, over the lives of more than two hundred thousand citizens of this Nation is incompatible with American ideals of liberty. It also is destructive of the character and self-respect of a great race.
>
> The continued application of the allotment laws, under which Indian wards have lost more than two-thirds of their reservation lands, while the costs of Federal administration of these lands have steadily mounted, must be terminated.
>
> Indians throughout the country have been stirred to a new hope. They say they stand at the end of the old trail. Certainly, the figures of impoverishment and disease point to their impending extinction, as a race, unless basic changes in their conditions of life are effected.
>
> I do not think such changes can be devised and carried out without the active cooperation of the Indians themselves.
>
> The Wheeler-Howard Bill offers the basis for such cooperation. It allows the Indian people to take an active and responsible part in the solution of their own problems.[43]

Thus the same government that had sought to abolish Indian self-government now proclaimed such a move contrary to "fundamental rights of political liberty" and believed that the Indians themselves had a part in their own salvation. Perhaps not surprisingly, part of the reasoning was the cost of administering to the Indians.

The Wheeler-Howard Act did not mean that the U.S. government had given up on complete absorption of the Indian nations. It just meant that the government recognized that allotment had failed. Assimilation was still the goal.

> The Wheeler-Howard Act, the most important piece of Indian legislation since the eighties, not only ends the long, painful, futile effort to speed up the normal rate of Indian assimilation by individualizing tribal land and other capital assets, but it also endeavors to provide the means, statutory and financial, to repair as far as possible, the incalculable damage done by the allotment policy and its corollaries.[44]

Likewise, the recognition of tribal governments was not a recognition of those governments that had been abolished, but rather extension of self-government by provisions to

> ... authorize and legalize tribal organization and incorporation, which give these tribal organizations and corporations limited but real power, and authority over their own affairs . . . .[45]

Indian nations which incorporated under the Wheeler-Howard Act or the Oklahoma Indian Welfare Act were not only recognized as having limited self-government, but could also receive various benefits under the act, including loans. The majority of Indian nations recognized by the U.S. government today were incorporated under these acts.

Opposition to the Wheeler-Howard Act was immediate and vociferous, but World War-II delayed substantive reaction. Those opposing the Wheeler-Howard Act, and those favoring assimilation in general, found a lot of ammo for their cause in the Second World War. There were around 25,000 Native Americans in uniform at the end of the war.[46] Their impressive service record included two Medals of Honor, 34 Distinguished Flying Crosses, 51 Silver Stars, 47 Bronze Stars and 71 Air Medals.[47] These men had proven their ability and deserved complete citizenship according to those opposed to the Wheeler-Howard Act. Complete assimilation, particularly political absorption, was the goal. Indians had proven themselves "worthy" of this. Federal supervision of sufficiently "advanced" Indian nations was to be terminated.

> Whereas it is the policy of Congress, as rapidly as possible, to make Indians within the territorial limits of the United States subject to the same laws and entitled to the same privileges and responsibilities as are applicable to other citizens of the United States, and to grant them all of the rights and prerogatives pertaining to American citizenship; And
>
> Whereas the Indians within the territorial limits of the United States should assume their full responsibilities as American citizens: Now, therefore, be it
>
> resolved by the House of Representatives (the Senate concurring),
>
> That it is the sense of Congress that, at the earliest possible time, all of the Indian tribes and Individual numbers thereof located within the states of . . . and all of the following named tribes, should be freed from Federal supervision and control and from all the disabilities and limitations specially applicable to Indians . . . [A]ll offices of the Bureau of Indian Affairs in the States of. . . . should be abolished. . . .[48]

Termination failed almost before it began. The first tribe to be terminated, the Menominee, were coerced into termination;[49] it was done too rapidly for appropriate planning; and, in the end, there was another mass transfer of tribal assets away from tribal members. The supposed boon of becoming "Americans" had again worked out to the detriment of the Native Americans.

> The "paper" genocide of American Indians under the termination policy subjected the Eisenhower administration to much criticism. "Termination" itself, became an ambiguous word in federal Indian policy that signified the extinction of numerous things: tribal governments, allotments, reservations, Indian rights, treaty obligations. ...
>
> In retrospect the termination policy of the second Eisenhower administration was a failure.[50]

Tribes scheduled to be terminated, some having "voluntarily" requested it, began to work against termination. They were quickly joined by those Indian nations not on the termination list. For Native Americans it became a crusade. Though termination had slowed before the end of the 1950's and ended altogether in the mid 1960's, it was a word that inspired fear among Indian people for decades to come.[51]

In the same year that the Termination Act became law, another attempt was made to forcibly incorporate the Indian nations. Public Law 280[52] was a compromise to complete termination in which any state which could assume civil and criminal jurisdiction over the Indian nations within their borders without the consent of the Indian nations. State control was not to be complete however, as the trust status of reservation lands was not terminated. Because of this, the states could not tax these lands. States requesting jurisdiction thus had little or no additional tax base to draw on for the costs of law enforcement. Despite this drawback, the assumption of power over the Indian nations was enough to cause five states to be written directly into the legislation and several more to assume such authority later.

> The expansion of metropolitan areas near Indian reservations has increased the states' interest in regulating and exploiting residential and recreational development on trust land. States have been notably desirous of acquiring pollution and subdivision control. The discovery of substantial energy resources on reser-

vations, and consequent industrial development, have spurred similar state interest in regulating and taxing those activities.[53]

States assumed authority for their own benefit, often doing little to maintain law and order on the reservations after they assumed jurisdiction. The Omaha and Winnebago reservations of Nebraska were left with no law enforcement once Federal officers departed.[54] States were unhappy with the result because it did not give them all the powers they wanted, while forcing them either to pay for law enforcement or accept lawlessness within their borders. Though Eisenhower asked Congress to amend the bill to provide for Indian consultation, they did not do so.[55] Indian nations were thus forced to accept this assimilationist policy. It was not until 1968 that Congress would provide for consent as a part of the Civil Rights Act. Since that time, no Indian nation has consented to state jurisdiction.

The social changes started in the 1960's were as profound in Indian country as elsewhere. The emphasis switched back from assimilation to self-determination of Indian nations. As President Johnson stated in a 1968 special message to Congress on the problems of the American Indian,

> Mississippi and Utah—the Potomac and the Chattahoochee—Appalachia and Shenandoah . . . The words of the Indian have become our words—the names of our states and streams and landmarks.
>
> His myths and his heroes enrich our literature. His lore colors our art and our language. For two centuries, the American Indian has been a symbol of the drama and excitement of the earliest America.
>
> But for two centuries, he has been an alien in his own land.Relations between the United States Government and the tribes were originally in the hands of the War Department. Until 1871, the United States treated the Indian tribes as foreign nations.It has been only 44 years since the United States affirmed the Indian's citizenship: the full political equality essential for human dignity in a democratic society. . . .
>
> But political equality and compensation for ancestral lands are not enough. The American Indian deserves a chance to develop his talents and share fully in the future of our Nation. . . .
>
> The American Indian, once proud and free, is torn now between white and tribal values; between the politics and language

of the white man and his own historic culture. His problems, sharpened by years of defeat and exploitation, neglect and inadequate effort, will take many years to overcome. . . .

No enlightened Nation, no responsible government, no progressive people can sit idly by and permit this shocking situation to continue.

I propose a new goal for our Indian programs: A goal that ends the old debate about "termination" of Indian programs and stresses self-determination; a goal that erases old attitudes of paternalism and promotes partnership self-help. . . .

In our efforts to meet that responsibility, we must pledge to respect fully the dignity and the uniqueness of the Indian citizen.

That means partnership—not paternalism.

We must affirm the right of the first Americans to remain Indians while exercising their rights as Americans.

We must affirm their right to freedom of choice and self-determination. . . .[56]

Such sweeping changes would not occur immediately. Major legislation expanding Native American self-governance would only be enacted after the Johnson administration. Under Johnson, Titles II-VII of the Civil Rights Act of 1968[57] all dealt with Indian people and nations, but were mixed in their action. Title II §202 imposed most of the "Bill of Rights" of the U.S. Constitution on Indian nations to regulate their power over their members, and §203 did the same for *habeus corpus* protection. Title III set up a model code for courts of Indian offenses. Title IV required tribal consent for state assumption of jurisdiction, and §403 (a) even allowed retrocession for those states already under P.L. 280. Title V added "assault resulting in serious bodily injury" to the crimes that were originally created by the Major Crimes Act. Possibly the most welcome change was Title VI. It allowed legal counsel contracts between Indian nations and their lawyers to automatically go through in 30 days if the Bureau of Indian Affairs took no action. This keeps the B.I.A. from hampering the tribes function either through neglect or stonewalling on approval of these contracts. Title VII provided for publication of various helpful guides and documents including the treaties, so they would be available to protect Indian rights. Thus none of the elements of the Civil Rights Act of 1968 actually increased sovereignty or self-governance, though Title IV at least kept the power from being usurped by the states. Title II can only be viewed as an imposition of external laws, however well-intentioned, actually diminishing sovereignty.

Though court cases affecting sovereignty were mixed in the 1970's,[58] the sweeping changes outlined by Johnson and supported by his successors would be implemented in a string of legislation beginning in 1975 and culminating in 1994.[59] P.L. 93-638, the Indian Self-Determination and Education Assistance Act[60] allows Indian nations to act as government contractors, providing their own services. Indian nations receiving these "638 contracts" expect to receive a number of benefits. Monies that had gone to non-Indian contractors to provide these services now go to the Indian nation itself. Some of the monies for administering the programs now flow to the tribal government rather than the Bureau of Indian Affairs. But perhaps most importantly, the Indian Nations provide their own services, knowing their own needs; sympathetic to their own problems; cognizant of their own customs.

Though a watershed change in policy, self-determination contracts are still much like any other U.S. Government contract. It is still the Federal Government that determines the needs to be met and the programs to meet them. The initiative possible under these contracts is severely limited. P.L. 103-413, Title II, the Self-Governance Act[61] changes this by allowing Indian nations to "compact" rather than contract these services. Compacting is considered as a government-to-government agreement in which the Indian nation takes over responsibility for various services. By compacting they can have all of the benefits of 638 contracts along with greater initiative. *Trying a New Way: The Independent Assessment Report on the Self-Governance Demonstration Project* outlined a number of benefits of self-governance including, better law enforcement; improved quality of tribal services; remarkable flexibility in meeting needs; facilitation of long-range planning; increased responsibility and accountability for tribal officials; better record management and accounting; increased participation of tribal members in priority setting; more efficient utilization of resources; quicker response to changing needs; consolidation of programs; and revision of tribal budgeting, organization, administration and government.[62]

Most importantly, under these acts, the U.S. Government has committed itself to a particular view of the relationship between the Federal Government and the Indian nations.

> The Congress, after careful review of the Federal Government's historical and special legal relationship with, and result-

ing responsibilities to, American Indian people, finds that—

(1) the prolonged Federal domination of Indian service programs has served to retard rather than enhance the progress of Indian people and their communities by depriving Indians of the full opportunity to develop leadership skills crucial to the realization of self-government, and has denied to the Indian people an effective voice in the planning and implementation of programs for the benefit of Indians which are responsive to the true needs of Indian communities; and

(2) the Indian people will never surrender their desire to control their relationships both among themselves and with non-Indian governments, organizations, and persons.[63]

With this view in mind, the U.S. Government committed itself to a particular policy.

Congressional declaration of policy

(a) Recognition of obligation of United States

The Congress hereby recognizes the obligation of the United States to respond to the strong expression of the Indian people for self-determination by assuring maximum Indian participation in the direction of educational as well as other Federal services to Indian communities so as to render such services more responsive to the needs and desires of those communities.

(b) Declaration of commitment

The Congress declares its commitment to the maintenance of the Federal Government's unique and continuing relationship with, and responsibility to, individual Indian tribes and to the Indian people as a whole through the establishment of a meaningful Indian self-determination policy which will permit an orderly transition from the Federal domination of programs for, and services to, Indians to effective and meaningful participation by the Indian people in the planning, conduct, and administration of those programs and services. In accordance with this policy, the United States is committed to supporting and assisting Indian tribes in the development of strong and stable tribal governments, capable of administering quality programs and developing the economies of their respective communities.[64]

Perhaps most interesting is the official U.S. Government statement concerning the origin of Indian nation governmental powers.

(3) Congress, through statutes, treaties, and the exercise of administrative authorities, has recognized the self-determination, self-reliance, and inherent sovereignty of Indian tribes;

(4) Indian tribes possess the inherent authority to establish their own form of government, including tribal justice systems.[65]

Thus since the mid 1990's, Indian people have been technically viewed as having inherent sovereignty, the inherent authority for self-government through their respective Indian nations despite their imposed U.S. citizenship. The statements of the United States Government appear to be sincere and forceful in the defense of Indian sovereignty, codified into law. But the U.S. pledged itself in hundreds of prior treaties and laws, repudiating each in turn to the detriment of Indian people and their nations. From the informal breaking of treaties done by individual Americans to their legal repudiation by solemn act of Congress, the laws of the United States have only protected Indian nations intermittently and poorly. They have as often served to destroy them. At the present time, bills are introduced in every session of Congress to do away with all or some of the laws protecting Indian nations. Just one Senator in the 105th Congress introduced five bills that would have limited tribal sovereign immunity.[66] If history is any indication, it is only a matter of time before such legislation is passed and the attitudes behind them again become official policy.

Notes

1. "The Outrage of Allotment" from *Conditions in Indian Territory,* Senate Committee Investigation, Senate Report no. 5013. 59th Cong., 2nd sess., Pt. 1. November 1906. Excerpted from its quote in Peter Nabokov, *Native American Testimony: A Chronicle of Indian-White Relations from Prophecy to the Present, 1492–1992,* (New York: Penguin, 1991),

266–267.

2. Extracted from the Board of Indian Commissioners, *Annual Report,* 1885, 90–91, citation contained in Angie Debo, *And Still the Waters Run: The Betrayal of the Five Civilized Tribes,* (Princeton: Princeton University, 1940; reprint Norman and London: University of Oklahoma, 1989), 21–22.

3. Extracted from the Board of Indian Commissioners, *Annual Report,* 1886. House Executive Document no. 1 49th Cong., 2nd sess., serial 2467, 81–82, 86–88 citation contained in Prucha, *Documents of U.S. Indian Policy,* 169–170.

4. Ibid., 171.

5. Gates, president of the Lake Mohonk Conference, is quoted in, James Wilson, *The Earth Shall Weep: A History of Native America,* (New York: Grove, 1998), 299.

6. H. Rept. No. 1576, May 28, 1880, 46th Cong., 2nd sess., 10. As quoted by Cohen, 209.

7. James Richardson, ed., vol. 7, pp 5239–5243.

8. *U.S. Statutes at Large,* 24:388.

9. TREATY WITH THE CHOCTAW {1830, Sept. 27} 7 Stat., 333. Proclamation, Feb. 24, 1831. Article 4 expressly forbids allotment. For text, see Appendix D , number 5.

10. *U.S. Statutes at Large,* 26:81.

11. Angie Debo, *The Rise and Fall of the Choctaw Republic,* The Civilization of the American Indian Series vol. 6, (Norman and London: University of Oklahoma, 1961), 184.

12. From *Senate Miscellaneous Document* no 24, 53rd Cong., 3rd sess., serial 3281, pp 8–12 as quoted by Prucha, *Documents of U.S. Indian Policy,* 191.

13. *U.S. Statutes at Large,* 30:495.

14. Francis E. Leupp, *The Indian and His Problem* (IP 1910), 336–337. As quoted in Cohen, 429–430.

15. Debo, *And Still the Waters Run,* 163–164.

16. *U.S. Statutes at Large,* 34:267, as amended 34:1286.

17. Richardson, vol. 10, p. 7438.

18. Reference in footnote 2 on page 95.

19. Rennard Strickland, "Genocide-At-Law: An Historical and Contemporary View of the Native American Experience," 34 *U. Ks. L. Rev.* 733.

20. John R. Wunder, *Retained by the People: A History of American Indians and the Bill of Rights,* (New York and Oxford: Oxford University, 1994), 33.

21. Hearings, Committee on Indian Affairs, 73rd Cong., 2nd sess., on

H.R. 7902, p 15–18. Extracted from citation by Cohen, 216. Various authors have quoted this as coming from William Brophie and Sophie Aberle, *The Indian: America's Unfinished Business*, (Norman, University of Oklahoma, 1966), 20, though Brophy and Aberle cited Cohen.

22. Ibid.

23. Remarks on the Indian Reorganization Act by Edgar Howard of Nebraska, *Congressional Record*, June 15, 1934, vol. 78, part 11, 73rd Cong., 2nd sess., p 11726. As cited by Carter Blue Clark, "The New Deal for Indians," *Between Two Worlds*, ed. by Arell Morgan Gibson, The Oklahoma Series vol. 22, (Oklahoma Historical Society, 1986), 73.

24. I cannot help but note here that my family received about 3,000 acres altogether under allotment of which only about 100 acres are still owned by the family today.

25. *Lone Wolf v. Hitchcock* 187 U.S. 553 (1903). For an excellent account of this case, see Blue Clark, *Lone Wolf v. Hitchcock: Treaty Rights and Indian Law at the End of the Nineteenth Century*, Law in the American West vol. 5, (Lincoln and London: University of Nebraska, 1994).

26. TREATY WITH THE KIOWA AND COMANCHE [1867, Oct. 21, 15 Stat.,81. Ratified. July 25, 1868. Proclaimed, Aug. 25. 1868.

27. This position was slowly relaxed over time, but the courts still only exercise limited review over Congress's plenary authority.

28. *Lone Wolf v. Hitchcock*, Ibid., 553–568.

29. An ironic appellation suggested by Choctaw Chief Allen Wright. The name means "red people" in the Choctaw language.

30. Administration of the Indian Office (Bureau of Municipal Research Publication no. 65, 1915), 17. As cited by Cohen, 155.

31. *U.S. Statutes at Large*, 43:253.

32. Allegiance was a key citizenship issue around the world as well as in the U.S., see *United States v. Wong Kim Ark*, 169 U.S. 649 (1898). Pages 655–658 discuss this issue giving numerous international precedents.

33. *Elk v. Wilkins*, 112 U.S. 94. (1884), 102.

34. *U.S. Statutes at Large*, 24:388, §6.

35. The Indian Citizenship Act and dual allegiance are the topics of Alexandra Witkins, "To Silence a Drum: The Imposition of United States Citizenship on Native Peoples", *Historical Reflections/Réflexions Historiques*, (New York: Alfred University, 1995), vol. 21, no. 2, 353–383.

36. These are common elements of the discussion of the Indian Citizenship Act, however all appear and are documented in Linda S. Parker, "The Indian Citizenship Act of 1924," *Between Two Worlds: The Survival of Twentieth Century Indians*, ed. by Arrell Morgan Gibson, The Oklahoma Series vol. 22, (Oklahoma Historical Society, 1986), 44–71.

37. Prucha, Great Father, Chapters 27 and 32 examine the Indian

schools and particularly the boarding schools, as does Frederick E. Hoxie, *A Final Promise: The Campaign to Assimilate the Indians, 1880-1920,* (Lincoln and London: University of Nebraska, 1984), chapter 6.

38. Commissioner Burke implemented reforms in 1929, see Prucha, *The Great Father,* 929, but the charges of cruelty in the system continued.

39. Removal of children from the state or territory of the parents without their consent was made illegal by *U.S. Statutes at Large* 28:906, and coercion in transferring students was made illegal by *U.S. Statutes at Large* 29:348.

40. *The Problem of Indian Administration,* (Baltimore: Johns Hopkins, 1928), as cited by Prucha, *The Great Father,* 838.

41. *U.S. Statutes at Large,* 48:948.

42. *U.S. Statutes at Large,* 49:1967.

43. Samuel Rosenman, ed., *Public Papers and Addresses of Franklin D. Roosevelt, 1934,* (New York: Random House, 1938), 202. Item 67, Statement on the Wheeler-Howard Bill.

44. *Annual Report of the Secretary of the Interior,* 1934, 78-83 extracted from a quote in Prucha, *Documents of U.S. Indian Policy,* 225.

45. Ibid., as quoted by Prucha at 227.

46. U.S. Office of Indian Affairs, *Indians in the War,* (Lawrence Kansas: Haskell Printing Department, 1945), 1 gives conservative figures totaling 24,551 for enlisted and non-commissioned officers, with the vast majority serving in the Army. The total number of officers was unknown. . Billy Hester, the author's uncle, was one of the relatively small number of Indians in the U.S. Navy. He served as an antiaircraft gunner assigned to merchant ships during the war.

47. Ibid.

48. *U.S. Statutes at Large,* 67:B132

49. See Prucha, *The Great Father,* 1050.

50. Donald L. Fixico, "Termination and Relocation: Federal Indian Policy in the 1950's" (PhD. diss., University of Oklahoma, 1980), 230.

51. An entertaining, short, account of termination can be found in Deloria, *Custer Died for Your Sins,* Ibid., chapter 3, .

52. *U.S. Statutes at Large,* 67:588.

53. Carole E. Goldberg, "Public Law 280: The limits of State Jurisdiction Over Reservation Indians", 22 U.C.L.A. L.Rev., 535 (1975). This article also provides a fine overview of the law, its causes and effects.

54. Goldberg, 552. Section B, 551-558 examines the problem of financing state jurisdiction including law enforcement.

55. Prucha, *The Great Father,* 1045.

56. Warren Reed, ed., *Public Papers of the Presidents of the United States: Lyndon B. Johnson, 1968-69,* (Washington D.C.: Government

Printing Office, 1970), item 113, 335–344.

57. *U.S. Statutes at Large,* 82:77–81.

58. Charles F. Wilkinson, *American Indians, Time, and the Law: Native Societies in a Modern Constitutional Democracy,* (New Haven and London: Yale, 1987), 59–62 discusses the contradictory cases of this period. In the end the courts relied on the notion of inherent sovereignty, mirroring the legislative initiatives being advanced, so a detailed discussion of these cases is unimportant. However, the fact that they occurred is just another example that the law is in flux and the status of Indian sovereignty is far from certain.

59. The most important, in order of passage are, P.L. 93–638, Jan 4th 1975, known as the "Indian Self-Determination and Education Assistance Act"; *U.S. Statutes at Large* 88:203. P.L. 100–472, Oct. 5th 1988; *U.S. Statutes at Large* 102:2298, particularly Title III, known as the "Self-Governance Demonstration Project"; P.L. 101-644, Nov. 29th 1990, *U.S. Statutes at Large* 104:4665; P.L. 103-176, Dec. 3, 1993, *U.S. Statutes at Large* 107:2004, known as the "Indian Tribal Justice Act"; P.L.103-413 Oct 25th 1994, *U.S. Statutes at Large* 108:4270, particularly Title II, known as the "Self-Governance Act".

60. *U.S. Statutes at Large* 88:203.

61. *U.S. Statutes at Large* 108:4270. Elements of this were originally tried on a temporary basis under P.L. 100-472, Oct. 5th 1988, *U.S. Statutes at Large* 102:2298, Title III, known as the Self-Governance Demonstration Project.

62. The Center for the Study of Indian Law and Policy, the University of Oklahoma and The Center for Tribal Studies, Northeastern State University, Tahlequah, *Trying a New Way: The Independent Assessment Report on the Self-Governance Demonstration Project,* (GPO, 1991), VII–VIII..

63. *U.S. Code,* Title 25, Chapter 14, Subchapter II, §450.

64. *U.S. Code,* Title 25, Chapter 14, Subchapter II, §450a.

65. *U.S. Code,* Title 25, Chapter 38, §3601. Other references to inherent sovereignty or authority of all or specified tribes are found in the texts of §1300f, §1301, §2501, §3602, §3631 and in the notes of §458aa, §1300f and §1301 all in their respective chapters of Title 25.

66. Senator Slade Gorton introduced S.1691, S.2298, S.2299, S.2301 and S.2302 for this purpose.

CHAPTER 6
A Case for Sovereignty

> *In the Government you call civilized, the happiness of the people is constantly sacrificed to the splendors of empire. Hence the origin of your codes of criminal and civil laws; hence your dungeons and prisons. We have no prisons; we have no pompous parade of courts; we have no written laws; and yet judges are as highly revered among us as they are among you, and their decisions are as much regarded.*
>
> *We have among us no exalted villains above the control of our laws. Daring wickedness is here never allowed to triumph over helpless innocence. The estates of widows and orphans are never devoured by enterprising swindlers.*
>
> *We have no robbery under the pretext of law.*
>
> —Joseph Brant, *Thayendanegea*, Mohawk[1]

It is clear from the history of Federal Indian law and policy that many of the problems of modern Native Americans were directly caused by the United States Government. Whatever the legality or morality of what happened, on the most conservative account, Native American people were divested of a continent; deprived of their independent governments; deprived of their cultures and physically decimated. On the surface, there is certainly a link between sovereignty and how Indian people have fared over the last two-hundred years. As sovereignty has been infringed, Indian people have been harmed; as sovereignty has been reaffirmed they have recovered.

The clearest link between the problems faced by Native Americans and the actions of the United States is the direct one of dispossession. Historical infringements of Indian sovereignty have coincided with dispossession that directly caused most or all of the harm. There is still a link to sovereignty however, as the eras of greater sovereignty saw improvements in conditions despite the fact that the real losses caused by direct actions were either not compensated for, or were poorly compensated for. Thus to account for improvements in eras of greater sovereignty one must look to sovereignty itself and not just a lack of exploitation. In addition, the recent Federal policy of self-governance recognizes the commonsensical view that people often know their own problems and needs best. This would, at least in part, explain why eras of increased sovereignty have been so positive—further strengthening the idea that sovereignty itself is important.

A better case for the link between sovereignty and Indian well-being can be made by recalling the kinds of problems faced by Indian people as outlined in Chapter One. Dispossession may account in part for the poverty, and the poverty may account in part for alcoholism and poor educational achievement but it cannot account for all of it. Education in particular provides a link to policies affecting sovereignty. Though college attendance is limited by ability to pay, education through high school is available to all Indian people regardless of their relative poverty. Yet, they often do not take advantage of it. Thus some factor or factors besides poverty must be important.

As seen in Chapter One, locus of control was the key factor that showed up repeatedly in explanations of poverty, alcoholism and lack of educational motivation. People who believe that they are not in control of their own lives are likely to suffer from these problems. Statistically, Indian people are apt to believe that they are not in control of their own lives.

The history of Federal Indian law and policy provides a clear and convincing reason for this. As demonstrated in Chapters Two through Five, this history is one in which Indian nations were slowly deprived of their lands and independence despite their best efforts to the contrary. Indian nation governments have been recognized, not recognized, abolished, re-instated, lionized and despised with little regard to their actual function. The Federal Government of the United States claims the legal right, through the plenary power doctrine, to complete control over Indian nation governments and it has the power to enforce this claim. This legal claim is bolstered by a claim of guardianship/trust authority that extends the claim down to individual Indian people as members of their respective nations.

Recent laws that recognize the inherent and retained sovereignty of Indian nations represent the culmination of long years of work on the part of Native American people, their nations and sympathizers. Though these laws are currently in force, the claim of plenary power remains. Continued challenges to Indian sovereignty, particularly in the context of this claim of Federal power and its history of use, make the current laws appear tenuous. Though some might argue that the current state of law empowers Native Americans to take control of their own destiny, hundreds of years of history have taught them otherwise.

If the current laws empowering Indian people were to continue as long in the future as the contradictory laws extend into the past, we might expect some of the ills engendered by history to be overcome. Eventually Native American people might again believe themselves to be the masters of their own fate. But this leaves the source of the problems untouched for generations, likely ensuring their continuation. This statement of the issue is also somewhat disingenuous. Given the history, Native American doubts as to the sincerity of current policy and uncertainty about its future are far from unreasonable. If anything, it would be unreasonable to expect them to believe that the current trend of self-governance will continue.[2]

If external locus of control, manifest in the Indian case as loss of sovereignty, is a significant factor in many of the problems of Indian people, then we finally have a clearer idea about why these problems seem so intractable. U.S. Government programs have been unable to solve the problems because of the fact that they *are* U.S. Government programs. Whether administered by the Indian nations as 638 contracts or under self-governance compacts, the spectre of Federal control remains. Congress still claims plenary power—the ultimate threat to Indian sovereignty. Though theorists like Wilkinson believe that the plenary power doctrine is not as all-powerful as is often claimed, their positions are like theories meant to persuade and don't really touch on the most problematic elements of plenary power.[3] The reality lies in cases like *United States v. Wheeler* in which the Supreme Court ruled, "The sovereignty that the Indian tribes retain is of a unique and limited character. It exists only at the sufferance of Congress and is subject to complete defeasance."[4]

The U.S. Government has made great strides toward relinquishing control, but even if they are sincere they would still have to convince the Indian people of this for the locus of control problem to be solved. The U.S. Government seems to have accepted the rightness of Indian self-governance. The question then is how to establish the *bona fides*. The obvious answer to this question is that the Federal Government specifically renounce plenary power and those elements of the trust/guardian relationship that provide control over Indian people as opposed to a mere duty to protect Indian people and their resources from others.

If one accepts the link between locus of control and the well being of Native Americans and if they are at all motivated to enhance Indian well being, then they should be in favor of relinquishment of Federal plenary power.

Renunciation of plenary power would not only be a key element in solving the problems faced by Native Americans, but it would bring them closer to having true sovereignty. The U.S. Government recognizes the inherent and retained sovereignty of Indian nations, but it is unclear just how this differs from self-determination or self-governance. If there is a difference, and if the Federal Government is committed to the sovereignty of Indian nations, then the policy should be something other than just self-determination or self-governance though these are the names for the policy initiatives prevailing today. These words have been used more-or-less interchangeably in this work so far. Now we shall have provide a short account differentiating sovereignty from the other terms.

A thorough analysis of sovereignty would be a topic requiring volumes, but for our purposes that is unnecessary. We are only concerned here with what sovereignty amounts to within the framework of U.S. law and political philosophy. Though self-determination and self-governance may describe limited powers of self-government, sovereignty is generally characterized as, "supreme, absolute and uncontrollable."[5] U.S. Government recognition of the inherent sovereignty of Native American nations would seem to conflict directly with Congressional plenary power under such a definition. Clearly the power of Indian nations is neither supreme nor absolute if Congress has plenary power.

But sovereignty is as much or more about the *source* of these powers and the *right* of their employ. This aspect of sovereignty is characterized as, "the self sufficient source of political power. . . the absolute right to govern."[6] This second element of sovereignty is essential to understanding the U.S. form of "divided" sovereignty. Individual states in the U.S. are spoken of as sovereign despite the fact that they are in many ways subordinate to the Federal Government. If the sovereignty of Indian nations can be accounted for within this system, then Federal pronouncements of Indian sovereignty do not contradict their claim of plenary power.

The American form of sovereignty is a departure from the old idea of absolute, indivisible sovereignty, though those ideas still linger in the standard definitions of sovereignty. As Daniel Webster put it,

> The Sovereignty of government is an idea belonging to the other side of the Atlantic. No such thing is known in North America. Our governments are all limited. In Europe, sovereignty is of feudal origin, and imports no more than the state of the sovereign. It comprises his rights, duties, exemptions, prerogatives and powers. But with us, all power is with the people. They alone are sovereign; and they erect what governments they please, and confer on them such powers as they please. None of these governments is sovereign, in the European sense of the word, all being ordained by written constitutions. It seems to me, therefore, that we only perplex ourselves when we attempt to explain the relations existing between the general government and the several State governments, according to those ideas of sovereignty which prevail under systems essentially different from our own.[7]

On this standard view, the people of the United States acting through the constitutional conventions formed the Constitution which lays out which powers are held by the central government and the state governments.

> From these conventions, the constitution derives its whole authority. The government proceeds directly from the people; is 'ordained and established,' in the name of the people; and is declared to be ordained, 'in order to form a more perfect union, establish justice and insure domestic tranquillity, and secure the blessings of liberty to themselves and to their posterity.' The assent of the states, in their sovereign capacity, is implied, in calling a convention, and thus submitting that instrument to the people. But the people were at perfect liberty to accept or reject it; and their act was final. It required not the affirmance, and could not be negatived, by the state governments. The constitution, when thus adopted, was of complete obligation and bound the state sovereignties.[8]

Thus the states are said to be sovereign though their power is severely limited by the Federal Government. This is because the power of both the state and Federal Governments are derived from the same source: the people. The United States government, through the Constitution, is founded on the principle of popular sovereignty.

To recognize this view of sovereign authority, a group could be said to have sovereign *power* if and only if their power of self-government is unlimited, or is limited and or subservient only to group(s) of which they are a part and to whom they have voluntarily given the power. On this view, Indian nations would have true sovereignty only if they are limited by or subservient only to groups of which they are part and to whom they have voluntarily given power. Arguably neither of these conditions obtain. Indian people were involuntarily made citizens as described on pages 76–77 supra, making their group membership unclear; and they have never voluntarily relinquished their power—certainly not the plenary power Congress claims.

This account appears to fit the vague but powerful notion of federal "divided" sovereignty generally held in the United States. If one accepts it as a plausible account of sovereignty within the dominant political philosophy of the United States, then plenary power would appear to be incompatible with it. Thus, if the Federal Government really recognizes Indian sovereignty, it should relinquish plenary power as incompatible with its own political philosophy. Though later arguments will strengthen this view of sovereignty and the incompatibility of plenary power within it, perhaps the clearest argument for this position comes from a Supreme Court case that appears to agree with much of the reasoning and even applies it directly to an Indian related case.

In the 1991 case of *Blatchford v. Native Village of Noatak*[9] the Supreme Court examined various issues including the surrender of sovereign immunity by state and tribal governments. Part of their reasoning is based on the 1934 case *Principality of Monaco v. State of Mississippi*[10] which they quote at some length. The relevant portion of that case, also quoted in *Blatchford v. Noatak* reads:

> There is also the postulate that States of the Union, still possessing attributes of sovereignty, shall be immune from suits, without their consent, save where there has been 'a surrender of this immunity in the plan of the convention.' The Federalist, No. 81. The question is whether the plan of the Constitution involves the surrender of immunity when the suit is brought against a State, without her consent, by a foreign State. [11]

Thus it would appear that the Court recognizes that the powers of sovereignty, or at least sovereign immunity, can only be voluntarily surrendered by a sovereign. The Court goes on to apply this idea to states and Indian tribes, finding that the reasoning doesn't apply in the same way due to relevant differences between the two.

> Respondents argue that Indian tribes are more like States than foreign sovereigns. That is true in some respects: They are, for example, domestic. The relevant difference between States and foreign sovereigns, however, is not domesticity, but the role of each in the convention within which the surrender of immunity was for the former, but not for the latter, implicit. What makes the States' surrender of immunity from suit by sister States plausible is the mutuality of that concession. There is no such mutuality with either foreign sovereigns or Indian tribes. We have repeatedly held that Indian tribes enjoy immunity against suits by States, Potawatomi Tribe, supra, at 509, as it would be absurd to suggest that the tribes surrendered immunity in a convention to which they were not even parties. [12]

This shows that the Supreme Court recognizes not only the standard notion of popular sovereignty and it's authority to grant sovereign powers via convention; but also the fact that the Indian nations were not party to such a convention and thus cannot have granted such powers. Though the case refers only to sovereign immunity there seems to be no way of differentiating that particular power from other sovereign powers, and the court provided no such reasoning in this case. Indeed, the Supreme Court's ruling in the 1982 case *Merrion v. Jicarilla Apache Tribe*[13] refers somewhat less eloquently to the idea that sovereign power must be waived by the holder of sovereign authority, but makes it clear that this is true for all sovereign powers. Justice Thurgood Marshall writing for the majority, said of the various Federal, State, local and Indian Governments,

> Each of these governments has different attributes of sovereignty, which may also derive from different sources. These differences, however, do not alter the principles for determining whether any of these governments has waived a sovereign power through contract, and we perceive no principled reason for holding that the different attributes of Indian sovereignty require different treatment in this regard. Without regard to source, sovereign

power, even when unexercised, is an enduring presence that governs all contracts subject to the sovereign's jurisdiction, and will remain intact unless surrendered in unmistakable terms.[14]

Thus it would seem the courts recognize that all sovereign powers, not just immunity, must be delegated by the sovereign authority.

The requirement of "mutuality" in the *Blatchford v. Native Village of Noatak* decision seems not only to strengthen this, but it also seems to be pointing to the importance of group membership. Though the decision is unclear on this point, it may be in agreement with the previously presented idea that the forced nature of Indian citizenship in the United States precludes their being subsumed under U.S. sovereignty. These two requirements are however separate and either of them is sufficient to make Congressional plenary power inconsistent with Congressionally recognized inherent Indian sovereignty. So even if one does not accept the importance of group membership, the necessity of a grant by convention remains. Ultimately, if one takes U.S. law and political philosophy seriously, the U.S. Government has never had the authority to take away Indian powers of sovereignty. The authority to grant such power is inherent in the Indian nations alone.

The "sources" of plenary power are insufficient to overcome this kind of objection. The Commerce Clause of the Constitution is often cited as the source of Congressional plenary power. Indeed, it has been said that, "Today federal power over Indian affairs is accepted as tracing primarily to the Indian Commerce Clause . . ."[15] But given the U.S. position on sovereignty, this does not make sense. Clearly plenary power cannot exist if it is based on any element of the Constitution, since that document is the result of a convention that did not include Indian nations. Even if this argument could be overcome, the Commerce Clause seems insufficient for such a grant of power. As argued supra at 47–48, the Commerce Clause only purports to grant power to regulate commerce with the Indian tribes. Even after adding all the other powers that Congress wields with respect to foreign nations, Marshall's delineation of the powers of Congress with respect to Indian nations is certainly not plenary, though he deems them sufficient for all essential[16] purposes.

Nonetheless this kind of explanation has been given in cases like *Mackey v. Cox*, supra at 62, in which it appears that the court is citing the Commerce Clause as putting Indian nations "under the Constitution." Even ignoring the Constitution's lack of authority to transfer another sovereign's powers and its failure to mention anything like "plenary power," this position would still be absurd. If mere mention in the Constitution is sufficient to place a group "under the Constitution" and give Congress plenary power over the group, then the same Commerce Clause would give the U.S. Congress plenary power over every foreign nation.

The closest that one can come to finding a legitimate source for plenary power, one that recognizes popular sovereignty, is in the use of the trust/guardianship relation. As noted supra at 47–48 the court used such a justification in *United States v. Kagama* stating that, "From their very weakness and helplessness, so largely due to the course of dealing of the Federal Government with them and the treaties in which it has been promised, there arises a duty of protection, and with it the power." But this explicitly recognizes the United States itself as the source of the weakness prompting Federal guardianship. Such a justification, if taken seriously, would be a case of "might making right." Subjugation of another country, regardless of reason, would be taken to grant legitimate power over that country.

The Court's citation of treaties requiring such protection may be an attempt to use the sovereign authority of the Indian nations to justify Federal presumption of sovereign power, with the relevant treaties taking the role of constitutional convention. While it is plausible that treaties could convey sovereign powers, their use in this instance cannot be taken to grant plenary power. The key problem with such a position would be that it again uses the aggression of U.S. citizens and states to justify the Federal government's usurpation of sovereign powers. The fact that the aggressor and protector are but two parts of the same country is ironic. Such a case would be analogous to claiming that a Texas invasion of Mexico gives the U.S. authority to assume sovereign powers over Mexico because they have defense treaties with Mexico. It would certainly seem that the treaties mean the U.S. is supposed to keep Texas from invading, not allow the Federal government to take over in its stead.

Of course some people may be willing to grasp the nettle and say that might makes right. Some might even want to avoid the whole issue of Indian sovereignty by an outright claim of conquest. Though this position should by now be held in contempt by all, it has certainly been used in Indian affairs. As John Marshall wrote,

> ... The United States then have unequivocally conceded to that great and broad rule by which its civilized inhabitants now hold

this country. They hold, and assert in themselves, the title by which it was acquired. They maintain, as all others have maintained, that discovery gave an exclusive right to extinguish the Indian title of occupancy, either by purchase or by conquest . . .

. . . Conquest gives a title which the courts of the conqueror cannot deny, whatever the private and speculative opinions of individuals may be, respecting the original justice of the claim which has been successfully asserted . . .

However extravagant the pretension of converting the discovery of a country into conquest may appear; if it has been asserted in the first instance, and afterwards sustained; if a country has been acquired and held under it; if the property of the great mass of the community originates in it, it becomes the law of the land, and cannot be questioned . . . However this restriction may be opposed to natural right, and to the usages of civilized nations, yet, if it be indispensable to that system under which the country has been settled, and be adapted to the actual condition of the two people, it may, perhaps, be supported by reason, and certainly cannot be rejected by Courts of justice.[17]

These resounding phrases of Marshall were not meant to justify the taking of sovereign powers or the assumption of sovereign authority, at most they justified the taking of land. As quoted supra at 32–33 "discovery gave an exclusive right to extinguish the Indian title of occupancy, either by purchase or by conquest." Though conquest was cited as a means of extinguishing Indian title, it was never cited as a reason diminishing Indian sovereignty in any other way. As shown in the preceding chapter, a large segment of the history of Indian relations to the United States, the removal period, is characterized by takeover of Indian land with the Indians removing to new territories where they might be free to continue governing themselves. Though sovereign power within territory taken by the United States passed to the United States, the Indian nations did not lose their sovereign powers within any territory they still controlled or came to control. This was recognized by President Jackson in that part of his statement quoted supra at 38 in which he advised the Cherokee to, "emigrate beyond the Mississippi or submit to the laws of those States." It was recognized by McLean in his concurrence as quoted supra at 50, ". . . Indian tribes within our states should exchange their territories, upon equitable principles, or, eventually, consent to become amalgamated in our political communities." It seems clear in the

A Case for Sovereignty

statement of President van Buren quoted supra at 50, where he said that the territory they were removing to was "exempt from all intrusions by white men . . ."

Even the conquest of the land was taken to be problematic when you look at Marshall's words. Phrases like, ". . . whatever private and speculative opinions of individuals may be, respecting the original justice of the claim . . ." or "However extravagant the pretension of converting the discovery of a country into conquest may appear . . ." or "However this restriction may be opposed to natural right . . ." all seem to point to some serious misgivings on the part of the very Chief Justice whose decision asserts the use of conquest. The problem is that the taking of land, particularly the taking of land that threatens the sovereignty of another, is problematic within the legal philosophy of the United States.

Clearly the sanctity of property is central to the legal precepts of the United States. The importance of the sovereignty of others and how the sovereignty of others affects American understanding of the acceptability of conquest is something that took longer to work out. The problem is precisely the one that led to removal. If one annexes a territory that contains a people having sovereign authority, the annexation is an extension of power over them. However, under a system that recognizes the legitimacy of popular sovereignty, only those people in the territory to be annexed actually have the authority to grant such power. You cannot take power, only they can give it to you. In the United States, the Indian nations were forced to retreat to retain their sovereign powers, something the Federal Government encouraged. The actions of the U.S. during removal seem to show that the U.S. had a developing awareness of how their assertion of the importance of popular sovereignty could serve as a limitation on conquest.

Fittingly, U.S. President Woodrow Wilson was among the first persons to deny the right of conquest specifically on the grounds of self-determination of peoples.

> The adoption of Wilsonian principles marked a revolution in the moral stance adopted by the Allies, from one which regarded the territory of the enemy as legitimate spoils of war to one which claimed to view that territory in the context of the self-determination of its inhabitants; from one which relied upon the operation of the right of conquest to one which apparently repudiated its validity. . . .
>
> . . . the principle of self-determination runs directly counter

to the suggestion that states may acquire rights of sovereignty merely by virtue of conquest.[18]

Wilsonian principles have been almost universally accepted in a series of treaties, charters and other agreements.[19] Since 1945 conquest has been against settled international law.[20]

The fact that the modern prohibition on conquest is specifically based on the notion of self-determination and popular sovereignty which is a cornerstone of U.S. law and political philosophy, should give pause to anyone wishing to invoke conquest. Though it took some time for the consequences of accepting popular sovereignty to be fully understood, that does not mean that the outcome of U.S. acceptance of the principle should have been any different historically than it is now. Any claim that the United States has a right to sovereignty over Indian people on the basis of conquest is in contradiction to the American principle of popular sovereignty. As President Woodrow Wilson said,

> No peace can last, or ought to last, which does not recognize and accept the principle that governments derive all their powers from the consent of the governed, and that no right anywhere exists to hand peoples about from sovereignty to sovereignty as if they were property.[21]

Even if there were some way around the "might makes right" problem for asserting plenary grants of power in the treaties, it is implausible that the Indian nations have ever conveyed such power to Congress through them. As noted supra at 48, John Marshall said of the treaty clauses creating the guardianship relation, "This relation was that of a nation claiming and receiving the protection of one more powerful; not that of individuals abandoning their national character, and submitting as subjects to the laws of a master." Thus it is clear that the courts originally did not view the Indian nations as having granted plenary power through their acceptance of U.S. protection.[22] The fact that John Marshall, the originator of the trust/guardianship notion, should make this statement adds more force to it. But even if Marshall hadn't made the statement, it should be clear that a nation would not give up the very thing that they are wishing to protect by asking for protection. The Indian nations were seeking to assure their continued national existence, not convey the power to destroy themselves.

The fact that surrender of plenary power is tantamount to

national destruction should, in itself, be enough to show that Congress cannot have such power without contradicting the idea of popular sovereignty. Under popular sovereignty, sovereign powers must be granted by the people having sovereign authority. The United States, through all its branches, recognizes the inherent sovereignty of Indian nations. This appears to be recognition that they have such authority. If the United States recognizes such authority, then the only way the United States could have plenary power over the Indian nations is if the nations granted those powers. Under plenary power Indian sovereignty is said to be, "subject to complete defeasance."[23] This would mean that the Indian nations had granted the United States the power to deprive them of all powers, effectively ending their existence as nations. This is certainly implausible. In addition, it contradicts U.S. recognition that, ". . . the Indian people will never surrender their desire to control their relationships both among themselves and with non-Indian governments, organizations, and persons."[24] Thus it would seem that the commonly cited sources of plenary power cannot possibly have conveyed it.

The only remaining principle of United States' law advanced as somehow legitimately granting power over Indian nations, is the doctrine of discovery. That doctrine was explicitly invoked by Marshall in the 1823 *Johnson v. McIntosh* decision which was quoted at length, supra 32–33. Though it is cited only as giving the United States the right to extinguish the Indian title of occupancy, that right would seem to intrude on Indian sovereign powers. A sovereign, in possession of all sovereign powers, would have the right to dispose of their property in any way they please. The United States recognizes the inherent sovereignty of Indian nations and specifically recognizes that, prior to the appearance of Europeans the Indian nations were, ". . . in the quiet and uncontrolled possession of an ample domain."[25] In other words, prior to the advent of the Europeans, the Indian nations not only had complete sovereign authority but also had all sovereign powers. So, if the doctrine of discovery is cited as giving the United States the sole right to extinguish Indian title, then it clearly denies certain sovereign powers to the Indian nations. If this is a legitimate source of sovereign powers within the American system, then it is one that purports to convey sovereign powers without grant by the sovereign authority.

That this position is held by the Courts seems clear. As McLean wrote in his concurring opinion in *Worcester v. Georgia*,

> At no time has the sovereignty of the country been recognized as existing in the Indians, but they have been always admitted to possess many of the attributes of sovereignty. All the rights which belong to self government have been recognized as vested in them. Their right of occupancy has never been questioned, but the fee in the soil has been considered in the government. This may be called the right to the ultimate domain, but the Indians have a present right of possession.[26]

In this opinion, McLean seems to be saying that the Indian nations have all the attributes of sovereignty but the "fee" which is in the hands of the U.S. Government. The U.S. Government claims this fee through the doctrine of discovery as previously seen in *Johnson v. McIntosh*. This fee then gives the U.S. Government "ultimate dominion." The U.S. Government holds the fee, but what is a fee?

> A freehold estate in lands, held of a superior lord, as a reward for services, and on condition of rendering some service for it. The true meaning of the word "fee" is the same as that of "feud" or "fief," and in its original sense is taken in contradistinction to "allodium," which latter is defined as a man's own land, which he possesses merely in his own right, without owing any rent or service to any superior.[27]

In a sense then, the U.S. Government might be claiming to be the ultimate feudal overlord, the King or Queen who is sovereign. This is an odd position for a country that denies the divine right of kings and substitutes for it the sovereignty of the people. Though some of the old sense of "domain" and "fee" undoubtedly colored the views of officials of the time, the more defensible position would be to say that the U.S. was imposing its version of land tenure. This is also more in keeping with the historical development of the doctrine of discovery, which will be examined shortly.

Without hearkening back to feudalism, it is hard to see how the United States could claim something like plenary power on the basis of the doctrine of discovery. All the doctrine of discovery purports to do is restrict the Indian sovereign power to convey (or not to convey . . .) the land to whom they please. Nonetheless this seems to be an essential element of the claim within cases like *United States v. Kagama*, quoted supra 64. In examining the sources of plenary power there, the court said, "But they [the United States] asserted an ultimate title in the land itself, by which the Indian tribes were forbidden to sell or to transfer it to other nations or peoples without the consent of this paramount authority."

Though it is doubtful that the doctrine of discovery implies plenary power, it still presumes to transfer sovereign powers without any grant by the sovereign authority: the Indian people. Can this transfer of power make sense under the American system of popular sovereignty?

The most thorough analysis of the doctrine of discovery is Robert A. Williams Jr.'s book, *The American Indian in Western Legal Thought*.[28] As Williams lays it out, the doctrine's development was long and complex. However, two main threads recur and appear to have been the basis of the United States claim: Religion and Lockean views of land tenure. As Williams wrote,

> Columbus's discoveries in the Crown's name were based on the presumption, affirmed in its essentials by Pope Alexander's bulls of donation, that Christian European discovery of territory held by infidel or pagan nonbelievers vested title in the discovering European nation.[29]

John Marshall's use of the doctrine of discovery in *Johnson v. McIntosh* appears to rely in part on the religious grounding of discovery. Laying out the discovery claim made by the Europeans and taken over by the United States, Marshall says,

> ... the character and religion of its inhabitants afforded an apology for considering them as a people over whom the superior genius of Europe might claim an ascendancy. The potentates of the old world found no difficulty in convincing themselves that they made ample compensation to the inhabitants of the new, by bestowing on them civilization and Christianity.[30]

Thus it would appear that part of the U.S. claim is based on religion. But this contradicts the supposedly secular nature of United States. Though it may not technically conflict with the 1st Amendment to the Constitution, it escapes only because it doesn't require any law to be passed. The United States has inherited the claims of the Europeans, which are fundamentally based on laws respecting an establishment of religion. This certainly breaks the spirit of the law, if not the letter. If we were to seriously accept discovery based on religion, then the land title of non-Christians in the United States and everywhere else in the world would be suspect. We cannot seriously consent to a law that would allow countries to "legitimately" take over other countries just because they are the "wrong" religion.

The other possible justification for the claim that discovery can convey sovereign power is its grounding in Lockean notions of property. Williams lays out part of this connection in sections entitled "Locke's Theory and the Indians' 'Wastelands'" and "Locke's Theory Applied: The Colonial Radicals' Praxis on the Indian Frontier."[31] On Williams' view, Locke's justification for taking of Indian land was not really part of the doctrine of discovery proper, but was more nearly the colonists' competing account. Either way, since the colonists are the ones who ultimately became the United States and established their ownership of the land via the doctrine of discovery, we can expect that it would be a part of their reasoning when applying the doctrine. On this account private property originates in labor. As Locke wrote,

> Thus this Law of reason makes the Deer, that *Indian's* who hath killed it; 'tis enough to be his goods who hath bestowed his labour upon it, though before, it was the common right of every one. And Amongst those who are counted the Civiliz'd part of Mankind, who have made and multiplied positive Laws to determine Property, this original Law of Nature for the *beginning of Property*, in what was before common, still takes place; and by vertue thereof, what Fish any one catches in the Ocean, that great and still remaining Common of Mankind; or what Ambergriese any one takes up here, is *by* the *Labour* that removes it out of the common state Nature left it in, *made* his *Property* who takes that pains about it. . . .[32]

Of course this is only the beginning of property. Eventually a system of land tenure can develop which limits what one may appropriate by labor. In Locke's words,

> 'Tis true in Land that is *common* in *England*, or any other Country, where there is Plenty of People under Government, who have Money and Commerce, no one can inclose or appropriate any part, without consent of all his Fellow-Commoners: Because this is left common by Compact, *i.e.* by the Law of the Land, which is not to be violated. And though it be Common in respect of some men, it is not so to all Mankind,

A Case for Sovereignty

but is the joint property of this Country, or this Parish. . . .[33]

Thus once a society develops a system of land tenure, property must be appropriated through that system—even if the property is part of the commons.

The following passage from the case *Johnson v. McIntosh*, makes it clear that this was a part of the idea of property applied in the United States.

> By the law of nature, they [the Indians] had not acquired a fixed property capable of being transferred. The measure of property acquired by occupancy is determined, according to the law of nature, by the extent of the men's wants, and their capacity of using it to supply them. . . . Upon this principle the North American Indians could have acquired no proprietary interest in the vast tracts of territory which they wandered over; and their right to the lands on which they hunted, could not be superior to that which is acquired to the sea by fishing in it. . . . According to every theory of property, the Indians had no individual rights to land; nor had they any collectively, or in their national capacity; for the land was not being used by them in such a manner as to prevent their being appropriated by a people of cultivators. . . . The right derived from discovery and conquest can rest on no other basis; and all existing titles depend on the fundamental title of the crown by discovery.[34]

But despite *Johnson v. McIntosh*, this kind of reasoning cannot justify assumption of sovereign powers over Indians because the reasoning cannot properly be applied to the Indian nations. Many Indian nations cultivated the land. Most American schoolchildren can tell you that Indian people were the originators of corn. Much more importantly though, the Indians had a system of land tenure and governments to go along with them. The U.S. Government recognized this every time they treated with a particular tribe for the cession of a particular piece of land. The U.S. Government even sought to destroy the system of common ownership used by most Indian nations by passing the General Allotment Act as described supra at 67–69. Thus it should be impossible for the United States to claim that the doctrine of discovery even applies to American Indians nations, much less that they can derive plenary power from it.

The applicability of *terra nullius*, Australian law's version of the doctrine of discovery, has been called into question on the same grounds. The relevant case, *Mabo v. Queensland*,[35] not only confirms the reasoning presented above, but it should lead us to consider some of the dynamics of striking down such laws.

> When British colonists went out to other inhabited parts of the world, including New South Wales, and settled there under the protection of the forces of the Crown, so that the Crown acquired sovereignty recognised by the European family of nations under the enlarged notion of terra nullius, it was necessary for the common law to prescribe a doctrine relating to the law to be applied in such colonies, for sovereignty imports supreme internal legal authority. . . . The view was taken that, when sovereignty of a territory could be acquired under the enlarged notion of terra nullius, for the purposes of the municipal law, that territory (though inhabited) could be treated as "desert uninhabited" country. The hypothesis being that there was no local law already in existence in the territory, the law of England became the law of the territory (and not merely the personal law of the colonists). . . . Ex hypothesi, the indigenous inhabitants of a settled colony had no recognised sovereign, else the territory could have been acquired only by conquest or cession. The indigenous people of a settled colony were thus taken to be without laws, without a sovereign and primitive in their social organisation. . . .
>
> The facts as we know them today do not fit the "absence of law" or "barbarian" theory underpinning the colonial reception of the common law of England. That being so, there is no warrant for applying in these times rules of the English common law which were the product of that theory. It would be a curious doctrine to propound today that, when the benefit of the common law was first extended to Her Majesty's indigenous subjects in the Antipodes, its first fruits were to strip them of their right to occupy their ancestral lands. Yet the supposedly barbarian nature of indigenous people provided the common law of England with the justification for denying them their traditional rights and interests in the land.
>
> . . . The theory that the indigenous inhabitants of a "settled" colony had no proprietary interest in the land thus depended on a discriminatory denigration of indigenous inhabitants, their social organisation and customs. . . .
>
> . . . If it were permissible in past centuries to keep the common law in step with international law, it is imperative in today's

world that the common law should neither be nor be seen to be frozen in an age of racial discrimination.

The fiction by which the rights and interests of indigenous inhabitants in land were treated as nonexistant was justified by a policy which has no place in the contemporary law of this country. . . .[36]

In this decision, Australia recognizes the injustice of laws like the doctrine of discovery. Thus it would seem that not only the sovereignty, but the very title to the land held by current Euro-Australians would be in question. Yet this is not so. In the remainder of its decision, the Australian Court finesses the issue by examining the basis of indigenous land tenure.

Native title has its origin in and is given content by the traditional laws acknowledged by and the traditional customs observed by the indigenous inhabitants of a territory. The nature and incidents of native title must be ascertained as a matter of fact by reference to those laws and customs. . . .

Of course, since European settlement of Australia, many clans or groups of indigenous people have been physically separated from their traditional land and have lost connection with it. . . . Where a clan or group has continued to acknowledge the laws and (so far as practicable) to observe the customs based on the tradition of that clan or group, whereby their traditional connection with the land has been substantially maintained, the traditional community title of that clan or group can remain in existence. . . . However, when the tide of history has washed away any real acknowledgement of traditional law and any real observance of traditional customs, the foundations of native title has disappeared. . . .[37]

But the "tides of history" did not wash away native tradition, the tides of Europeans did. The decision maintains the *status quo* of ownership and power as much as possible while recognizing the past injustice of *terra nullius*. However, in doing so it is effectively making might right again. If the discoverers can disrupt native communities enough to disrupt their social order, they can claim legal title. Though the *Mabo v. Queensland* decision strikes down an unjust law, it creates a new more complicated set of unjust doctrines that perpetuate their results.

The European colonial nations have become trapped by their

own sense of justice. As they have come to understand how their past actions conflict with their own sense of justice, they have called into question their own right to exist. A recognition of this problem goes all the way back to the beginning. As Marshall said in *Johnson v. McIntosh*,

> However extravagant the pretension of converting the discovery of a country into conquest may appear; if it has been asserted in the first instance, and afterwards sustained; if a country has been acquired and held under it; if the property of the great mass of the community originates in it, it becomes the law of the land, and cannot be questioned...[38]

Modern U.S. recognition of the inherent and retained sovereignty of the Indian nations must be seen in this light. The U.S. is attempting reconcile its right to exist with its own recognition of the injustices that gave it birth and nurtured it. The centrality of popular sovereignty to United States' law makes it impossible not to recognize the sovereignty of Indian nations. Thus something like the doctrine of inherent and retained sovereignty must exist. However, to retain its own sovereignty—its power, the United States has subordinated Indian sovereignty under a plenary power doctrine that again fails to recognize the real import of popular sovereignty.

The labyrinth of Indian law is necessary to hide the fact that the United States is violating its most fundamental principles:

> We hold these truths to be self-evident, that all men are created equal, that they are endowed by their Creator with certain unalienable Rights, that among these are Life, Liberty and the pursuit of Happiness.—That to secure these rights, Governments are instituted among Men, deriving their just powers from the consent of the governed.[39]

The doctrine of inherent and retained sovereignty under the plenary power of Congress is just the most recent turn in the labyrinth.

To the extent that inherent and retained sovereignty recognizes the right of Indian people to govern themselves, it is good. The empowerment of Indian people can help to overcome the problems linked to locus of control. Though plenary power stands in the way of immediate realization of the full benefits of this empowerment, it may be the best that can be gotten from the United States.

A Case for Sovereignty

If the doctrine could be maintained in the face of plenary power, it might be an acceptable pragmatic solution even though it does not fully recognize Indian sovereignty. Unfortunately, the inherent contradictions make the situation tenuous.

Indian people are seen as being a part of the United States, yet they are recognized as having an independent inherent sovereignty. Though the prerogatives that go along with this sovereignty are few and easily outweighed by the negatives that go along with Indian history, many Americans resent the prerogatives. As Louis Claiborne put it,

> ... for one untutored in Indian Law, the major decisions of the supreme court seem very questionable, if not downright "un-American."
>
> - Why should Indians enjoy special preferences in jobs and government contracts?
> - Why should Indian property and Indian Reservation income be uniquely exempted from State and local taxes, even when Indians receive some services paid for by those taxes?
> - Why should Indians who pay no state and local taxes be entitled to vote in state and local elections?
> - Why should tribal governments have the power to regulate and tax non-Indians on reservations on a Reservation who are ineligible to sit on the tribal council or to participate in the election of council members?
> - Why should Indians alone be free to hunt and fish free of most restrictions, except of their own choosing?
> - Why should relatively few Indians in the State of Washington be assured the right to catch half the salmon, while the other fishermen are compelled to share the other half?
> - Why should Indians have the unique right to preempt scarce water which, for the most part, they do not even use today?
>
> These, and like questions, challenge very fundamental principles, embodied in mottos that every schoolboy learns: "No taxation without representation," "government is color blind," "equality under the law," "one man one vote." Of course, there are special reasons for these exceptional rules. But I should not like the Court (or Congress) to be bound by the answers a Gallup poll would give these questions.[40]

As Claiborne points out, these questions stem from fundamental principles, principles as fundamental as that of popular sovereignty and much more well-known than the intricacies of Indian law. The current level of Indian sovereignty can't be maintained in the face of such objections. Either Indians are or are not a part of the United States. The U.S. Government claims they are and most Americans wouldn't even question it. Despite this the Government administers to its Indian citizens differently. If the Indian nations had been taken into the Union under a compact that defined these differences, then they would be straightforwardly laid out and would have been agreed to by the citizens of the United States. If they had been taken into the Union under a compact at all, differences or no, it would at least have made their sovereignty within the Federal system of divided sovereignty comprehensible. As it is, the compatibility of the fundamental principles of the United States with the laws that protect Indian sovereignty is at least as questionable as the compatibility of those fundamental principles with the laws that originally took away Indian sovereignty. While the fundamental principles supporting Indian sovereignty are hidden behind the intricacies and contradictions of Indian law, the same principles revealed in their full glory can be used to destroy Indian sovereignty.

The majority of American are completely unaware of the issues of Indian sovereignty. The only ones to whom these issues matter are the Indians and their sympathizers on one side and all the non-Indians who resent the "special treatment" of the Indians on the other side. In an era when affirmative action programs are in retreat, Indian sovereignty is certain to be in trouble.

Congressional renunciation of plenary power, or judicial revocation of it, would not solve the problem. The fundamental tensions in the remaining laws would still be there, as would the tensions between Indian society and the dominant society. However, the end of plenary power would eliminate the most objectionable of the vestiges of the old colonial system. Perhaps more importantly it would buy time and bring the issue to the attention of a broader public. If all the U.S. citizens who are not directly affected by Indian sovereignty were to consider the issues in the light of the fundamental principles of the United States, they might be truly recognize the inherent sovereignty of Indian nations. Congressional renunciation of plenary power would be dramatic and it would help show the way to understanding. It would buy time by denying Congress the ability to eliminate Indian sovereignty with the stroke of a pen when anti-sovereignty pressure mounts.

Indian people must understand that their sovereignty is a direct threat to the very existence of the United States—if only to its existence as a particular image in the mind of its people. If the U.S. truly recognized Indian sovereignty, it would be recognizing the illegitimacy of its origins. Thus the first move for Indian people must be to recognize the right of the United States to exist. To some, this may seem overly dramatic, but ultimately it is at the core of the problem. If plenary power is renounced, Indian nations will have much greater potential power. But it is power they must refrain from using until a compact can be made which recognizes their power and, possibly, freely grants the United States certain powers. Until that time, they must recognize and be bound by existing Indian law.

This idealistic dream is one that will probably never work. Too many people have vested interests in maintaining their power over Indian nations. Yet, it is the only one available and it may have some slim hope of succeeding. Euro-Americans have come a long way in the last two-hundred years. They renounced slavery in the 1860's and finally managed to get rid of the discriminatory laws that perpetuated many related injustices into the 1960's. Though they still have a long way to go on that issue, they have advanced. In the 1990's they finally codified a recognition of the inherent sovereignty of Indian nations. Perhaps before the end of the next century they can finally do away with the Indian law that perpetuates the original injustice.

"Government derives its just power from the consent of the governed," is not only the fundamental principle of U.S. Government, but among the greatest statements of moral truth ever made. Every American should be proud of this statement, but until Indian sovereignty has been truly recognized, that statement will ring hollow.

Notes

1. As quoted by Nerburn and Mengelkoch *Ibid.*, 78–79.
2. Though many specialists seem to think that this trend will continue. In a special feature in 22 *Am. Ind. L. Rev.*, (1999), 585–622, Louis F. Claiborne, Reid Peyton Chambers and Douglas B.L. Endreson, all wrote articles concluding that most major elements of Indian self-governance already in place would remain in force. Though there were no dissenting opinions presented, Claiborne did express some misgivings that will be enumerated infra at 111.
3. Charles F. Wilkinson, *American Indians, Time, and the Law: Native Societies in a Modern Constitutional Democracy*, (New Haven and London: Yale, 1987), his section entitled "The Higher Sovereign" on pages 78–89 sets out to show, among other things, that plenary power is not unlimited. But on page 79 he provides a litany of the worst "by-products" of plenary power saying, "None of these by-products of the plenary power doctrine has been shaken by the modern Court nor is any likely to be."
4. *United States v. Wheeler*, 435 U.S. 313, (1978), at 323.
5. Henry Campbell Black, *Black's Law Dictionary*, 6th edition by the publishers editorial staff, Joseph R. Nolan, Jacqueline M. Nolan-Haley, M.J. Connolly, Stephen C. Hicks, and Martina N. Alibrandi, (St. Paul: West Publishing, 1990), 1396.
6. Ibid.
7. Daniel Webster, *The Works of Daniel Webster*, volume III, (Boston: Charles C. Little and James Brown, 1851), 469. Charles F. Wilkinson, *American Indians, Time, and the Law*, Ibid., 54 quotes a portion of this, incorrectly attributing it to Thomas Jefferson. The cite for this quote, on page 172, uses the appropriate volume and page from Webster but attributes it to "The Works of Thomas Jefferson," a clear conflation with the Webster title. Wilkinson probably took this quote from C.E. Merriam, *History of the Theory of Sovereignty Since Rousseau*, Studies in History, Economics and Public Law Volume XII, Number 4, (New York: Columbia University, 1900). It correctly cites Webster on page 166, provides a slightly longer extract in the text, and extends the quote in a footnote just as Wilkinson did later.
8. *M'Culloch v. State of Maryland*, 17 U.S. 316 (1819), 403–404.
9. *Blatchford v. Native Village of Noatak*, 501 U.S. 775 (1991).
10. *Principality of Monaco v. State of Mississippi*, 219 U.S. 313 (1934).
11. Ibid., 322–323.
12. *Blatchford v. Native Village of Noatak*, Ibid., 782.

A Case for Sovereignty

13. *Merrion v. Jicarilla Apache Tribe*, 455 U.S. 130, (1982).
14. Ibid., 149.
15. David H. Getches, Charles F. Wilkinson and Robert A. Williams, Jr., *Federal Indian Law: Cases and Materials*, 3rd ed., (St. Paul: West Publishing, 1993), 326.
16. As quoted supra at 47, "These powers comprehend all that is required for the regulation of our intercourse with the Indians."
17. Extracted from the extended quotation supplied supra at 32–33.
18. Sharon Korman, *The Right of Conquest: The Acquisition of Territory by Force in International Law and Practice*, (Oxford: Clarendon Press, 1996), 139.
19. Ibid., Part Two: The Demise of the Right of Conquest in the Twentieth Century, pages 133-301 traces this evolution. In particular Chapter 6, pages 179–248, examines the legal elements of the demise of conquest.
20. W. Michael Reisman, the Myres S. McDougal Professor of International Law at Yale University, stated this unequivocally in a telephone conversation on March 4th, 1999.
21. Ray Stannard Baker and William E. Dodd, eds., *The Public Papers of Woodrow Wilson*, volume II (New York: Harper, 1926), 411. From a speech made January 22nd, 1917.
22. Some additional support for this is given in the surrounding text, supra 47–49.
23. As stated in *United States v. Wheeler*, quoted supra at 92.
24. *U.S. Code*, Title 25, Chapter 14, Subchapter II, §450, extracted from the extended quote provided supra at 84–5.
25. From John Marshall's opinion in *Cherokee Nation v. Georgia* quoted supra at 32.
26. *Worcester v. Georgia*, Ibid., 580.
27. Henry Campbell Black, *Black's Law Dictionary*, Ibid., 614.
28. Robert A. Williams, Jr., *The American Indian in Western Legal Thought*, (New York and Oxford: Oxford University, 1990).
29. Ibid., 99.
30. From the extended quote supra 32.
31. Robert A. Williams, Jr, American Indian in Western Legal Thought, Ibid., 246–251.
32. John Locke, *Two Treatises of Government,* II, §30. From the volume edited by Peter Laslett in the Cambridge Texts in the History of Political Thought series, (Cambridge and New York: Cambridge University, 1988). All quotes from this work are transcribed with emphasis punctuation and spelling as they appear in this edition.
33. John Locke, *Two Treatises of Government,* Ibid.,II, §35.

34. *Johnson v. McIntosh*, Ibid., 569–570. This segment even specifically cites Locke.

35. 107 A.L.R. 1 (1992) (Australian High Court). Quotations extracted here will be from Getches, Wilkinson and Williams, *Federal Indian Law*, Ibid., and will refer to pages in that volume.

36. Ibid., 1011–1012.

37. Ibid., 1013–1014.

38. Extracted from the extend quote supra at 33.

39. *The Declaration of Independence*

40. Louis F. Claiborne, "The Trend of Supreme Court Decisions in Indian Cases," 22 *Am. Ind. L. Rev.*, (1999), 587–588.

APPENDIX A
The Bureau of Indian Affairs Mission Statement

The Bureau of Indian Affairs' mission is to enhance the quality of life, to promote economic opportunity, and to carry out the responsibility to protect and improve the trust assets of American Indians, Indian Tribes and Alaskan Natives. We will accomplish this through the delivery of quality services, maintaining government-to-government relationships within the spirit of Indian self-determination.

APPENDIX B

Mission Statement of The Office of Indian Education Programs

Recognizing the special rights of Indian Tribes and Alaska Native entities and the unique government-to-government relationship of Indian Tribes and Alaska Native villages with the Federal Government as affirmed by the United States Constitution, U.S. Supreme Court decisions, treaties, Federal statutes, and Executive Orders, and as set out in the Congressional declaration in sections 2 and 3 of the Indian Self-Determination and Education Assistance Act (Pub. L. 93– 638; 88 Stat. 2203; 25 U.S.C. 450 and 450a), it is the responsibility and goal of the Federal government to provide comprehensive education programs and services for Indians and Alaska Natives. As acknowledged in section 5 of the Indian Child Welfare Act of 1978 (Pub. L. 95–608; 92 Stat. 3069; 25 U.S.C. 1901), in the Federal Government's protection and preservation of Indian Tribes and Alaska Native villages and their resources, there is no resource more vital to such Tribes and villages than their young people and the Federal Government has a direct interest, as trustee, in protecting Indian and Alaska Native children, including their education. The mission of the Bureau of Indian Affairs, Office of Indian Education Programs, is to provide quality education opportunities from early childhood through life in accordance with the Tribes' needs for cultural and economic well-being in keeping with the wide diversity of Indian Tribes and Alaska Native villages as distinct cultural and governmental entities. The Bureau shall manifest consideration of the whole person, taking into account the spiritual, mental, physical and cultural aspects of the person within family and Tribal or Alaska Native village contexts.

APPENDIX C
Mission Statement of the Indian Health Service

The IHS provides a comprehensive health services delivery system for American Indian and Alaska Natives with opportunity for maximum tribal involvement in developing and managing programs to meet health needs. The goal of IHS is to raise the health status of the American Indian and Alaskan Native people to the highest possible level.

To carry out its mission and to attain its goal, IHS (1) assists Indian tribes in developing their health programs through activities such as health management training, technical assistance, and human resource development; (2) facilitates and assists Indian tribes in coordinating health planning, in obtaining and utilizing health resources available through the Federal, State, and local programs, in operating comprehensive health care services, and in health program evaluation; (3) provides comprehensive health care services, including hospital and ambulatory medical care, preventative and rehabilitative services, and development of community sanitation facilities; and (4) serves as the principal Federal advocate for Indians in the field of health to ensure comprehensive health services for American Indian and Alaska Native people.

APPENDIX D

Treaty Excerpts

The following excerpts from treaties and agreements between the United States and various Indian nations show that the United States explicitly recognized various rights and attributes of Indian nations as laid out in the following key. Arguably every treaty, by its very nature, recognizes the sovereignty, independence, government, laws and jurisdiction of Indian nations. The treaties excerpted here represent only a small fraction of all the treaties made between the U.S. and the Indian nations.

All treaty excerpts taken from Charles J. Kappler, *Indian Treaties 1778–1883*, (Mattituck New York: Amereon House, 1972; reprint of *Indian Affairs: Treaties and Laws,* Volume II, Treaties, Washington D.C.: GPO, 1904).

Key

J: Explicit recognition of jurisdiction of Indian nation. Instances where an Indian nation is guaranteed to never be included in the jurisdiction of any territory or state of the union are included in this category.
C: Explicit recognition of Indian nation courts.
L: Explicit recognition of Indian nation laws/regulations.
P: Guarantee of Indian ownership in perpetuity of land.
G: Explicit recognition of Indian nation government.
R: Guarantees a perpetual right to self-government. Instances where there is a stipulation that U.S. laws do not interfere with Indian nation laws et cetera are taken to be of this sort.
O: Guarantees a perpetual right to ownership in-common

1. P
TREATY WITH THE WYANDOT, DELAWARE, OTTAWA, CHIPPEWA, POTTAWATIMA AND SAC NATIONS {1789, Jan. 9} 7 Stat., 28. Proclamation, Sept. 27, 1789.
... do by these presents renew and confirm the said boundary line; to the end that the same may remain as a division line between the lands of the United States of America, and the lands of said nations, forever.

2. J
TREATY WITH THE CHIPPEWA {1826, Aug. 5} Stat., 7, 290. Proclamation, Feb. 7, 1827.
ARTICLE 3. The Chippewa tribe grant to the government of the United States the right to search for, and carry away, any metals or minerals from any part of their country. But this grant is not to affect the title of the land, nor the existing jurisdiction over it.

3. J P
TREATY WITH THE WESTERN CHEROKEE {1828, May 6} 7 Stat., 311. Proclamation, May 2.8, 1828.
WHEREAS, it being the anxious desire of the Government of the United States to secure to the Cherokee nation of Indians, as well those now living within the limits of the Territory of Arkansas, as those of their friends and brothers who reside in States East of the Mississippi, and who may wish to join their brothers of the West, a permanent home, and which shall, under the most solemn guarantee of the United States, be, and remain, theirs forever a home that shall never, in all future time, be embarrassed by having extended around it the lines, or placed over it the jurisdiction of a Territory or State, nor be pressed upon by the extension, in any way, of any of the limits of any existing Territory or State . . .
ARTICLE 2. The United States agree to possess the Cherokees, and to guarantee it to them forever, and that guarantee is hereby solemnly pledged, of seven millions of acres of land, to be bounded as follows, viz . . .

4. P
TREATY WITH THE DELAWARES {1829, Sept. 24} 7 Stat., 327. Proclamation, Mar. 24, 1831.
... shall be conveyed and forever secured by the United States, to the said Delaware Nation, as their permanent residence: And the United States hereby pledges the faith of the government to guar-

antee to the said Delaware Nation forever, the quiet and peaceable possession and undisturbed enjoyment of the same, against the claims and assaults of all and every other people whatever.

5. J L P G R
TREATY WITH THE CHOCTAW {1830, Sept. 27} 7 Stat., 333. Proclamation, Feb. 24, 1831.
ARTICLE 2. The United States under a grant specially to be made by the President of the U. S. shall cause to be conveyed to the Choctaw Nation a tract of country west of the Mississippi River, in fee simple to them and their descendants, to inure to them while they shall exist as a nation and live on it . . .
ARTICLE 4. The Government and people of the United States are hereby obliged to secure to the said Choctaw Nation of Red People the jurisdiction and government of all the persons and property that may be within their limits west, so that no Territory or State shall ever have a right to pass laws for the government of the Choctaw Nation of Red People and their descendants; and that no part of the land granted them shall ever be embraced in any Territory or State; but the U. S. shall forever secure said Choctaw Nation from, and against, all laws except such as from time to time may be enacted in their own National Councils, not inconsistent with the Constitution, Treaties, and Laws of the United States; and except such as may, and which have been enacted by Congress, to the extent that Congress under the Constitution are required to exercise a legislation over Indian Affairs. But the Choctaws, should this treaty be ratified, express a wish that Congress may grant to the Choctaws the right of punishing by their own laws, any white man who shall come into their nation, and infringe any of their national regulations.

6. P
TREATY WITH THE SENECA, ETC. {1831, July 20} 7 Stat., 351. Proclamation, Apr. 6, 1832.
ARTICLE 2. In consideration of the cessions stipulated in the foregoing article, the United States agree to cause the said band of Senecas and Shawnees, consisting of about three hundred souls, to be removed in a convenient and suitable manner to the western side of the Mississippi river, and will grant by patent, in fee simple to them and their heirs forever, as long as they shall exist as a nation and remain on the same, a tract of land to contain sixty thousand acres, to be located under the direction of the President of the United States . . .

Appendix D 123

7. P
TREATY WITH THE KICKAPOO {1832, Oct. 24} 7 Stat., 391. Proclamation, Feb. 13, 1833.
. . . it is hereby agreed that the country within the following boundaries shall be assigned, conveyed, and forever secured, and is hereby so assigned, conveyed, and secured by the United States to the said Kickapoo tribe, as their permanent residence, viz . . .

8. P
TREATY WITH THE WESTERN CHEROKEE {1833, Feb. 14}7 Stat., 414. Proclamation, Apt. 12, 1834.
ARTICLE 1. The United States agree to possess the Cherokees, and to guarantee it to them forever, and that guarantee, is hereby pledged, of seven millions of acres of land, to be bounded as follows viz . . .

9. J L G R
AGREEMENT WITH THE CHEROKEE {1835, March 14} Unratified. Indian Office, box 1,Treaties 1802–1853. See Senate Doc. No. 120, 25th Congress, 2d session, p. 459.
ARTICLE 6. The United States hereby covenant and agree, that the lands ceded to the Cherokee nation, in the foregoing article, shall, in no future time, without their consent, be included within the territorial limits or jurisdiction of any State or Territory; but they shall secure to the Cherokee Nation the right, by their National Councils, to make and carry into effect all such laws as they may deem necessary for the government and protection of the persons and property within their own country, belonging to their people, or such persons as have connected themselves with them: Provided always, That they shall not be inconsistent with the Constitution of the United States, and such acts of Congress as have been or may be passed for the regulation of Indian affairs; and also, that they shall not be considered as extending to such citizens and Army of the United States, as may travel or reside in the Indian country, according to the laws and regulations established by the government of the same.

10. J L G R
TREATY WITH THE CHEROKEE {1835, Dec. 29} 7 Stat., 478. Proclamation, May 23, 1836.
WHEREAS the Cherokees are anxious to make some arrangements with the Government of the United States whereby the dif-

ficulties they have experienced by a residence within the settled parts of the United States under the jurisdiction and laws of the State Governments may be terminated and adjusted; and with a view to reuniting their people in one body and securing a permanent home for themselves and their posterity in the country selected by their forefathers without the territorial limits of the State sovereignties, and where they can establish and enjoy a government of their choice and perpetuate such a state of society as may be most consonant with their views, habits and condition; and as may tend to their individual comfort and their advancement in civilization.
ARTICLE 5. The United States hereby covenant and agree that the lands ceded to the Cherokee nation in the forgoing article shall, in no future time without their consent, be included within the territorial limits or jurisdiction of any State or Territory. But they shall secure to the Cherokee nation the right by their national councils to make and carry into effect all such laws as they may deem necessary for the government and protection of the persons and property within their own country belonging to their people or such persons as have connected themselves with them: provided always that they shall not be inconsistent with the constitution of the United States and such acts of Congress as have been or may be passed regulating trade and intercourse with the Indians; and also, that they shall not be considered as extending to such citizens and Army of the United States as may travel or reside in the Indian country by permission according to the laws and regulations established by the Government of the same.

11. P
TREATY WITH THE OTTAWA, ETC. {1836, Mar. 28} 7 Stat., 491. Proclamation, May 27, 1836.
ARTICLE 8. It is agreed, that as soon as the said Indians desire it, a deputation shall be sent to the southwest of the Missouri River, there to select a suitable place for the final settlement of said Indians, which country, so selected and of reasonable extent, the United States will forever guaranty and secure to said Indians.

12. P
TREATY WITH THE MIAMI {1838, Nov. 6} 7 Stat., 569 Proclamation, Feb. 8, 1839.
ARTICLE 10. The United States stipulate to possess, the Miami tribe of Indians of, and guarranty to them forever, a country west

Appendix D 125

of the Mississippi river, to remove to and settle on, when the said tribe may be disposed to emigrate from their present country, and that guarranty is hereby pledged: And the said country shall be sufficient in extent, and suited to their wants and condition and be in a region contiguous to that in the occupation of the tribes which emigrated from the States of Ohio and Indiana. And when the said tribe shall have emigrated, the United States shall protect the said tribe and the people thereof, in their rights and possessions, against the injuries, encroachments and oppressions of any person or persons, tribe or tribes whatsoever.

13. P O
TREATY WITH THE CHEROKEE {1846, Aug. 6} 9 Stat., 871. Ratified Aug. 8,1846. Proclaimed Aug. 17, 1846.
ARTICLE 1. That the lands now occupied by the Cherokee Nation shall be secured to the whole Cherokee people for their common use and benefit; and a patent shall be issued for the same, including the eight hundred thousand acres purchased, together with the outlet west, promised by the United States, in conformity with the provisions relating thereto, contained in the third article of the treaty of 1835, and in the third section of the act of Congress, approved May twenty-eighth, 1830, which authorizes the President of the United States, in making exchanges of lands with the Indian tribes, "to assure the tribe or nation with which the exchange is made, that the United States will forever secure and guarantee to them, and their heirs or successors, the country so exchanged with them; and if they prefer it, that the United States will cause a patent or grant to be made and executed to them for the same: Provided, always, That such lands shall revert to the United States if the Indians become extinct or abandon the same."

14. J C L P G R O
TREATY WITH THE CHOCTAW AND CHICKASAW {1855, June 22} 11 Stat., 611. Ratified Feb. 2 1, 1856. Proclaimed Mar. 4, 1856.
ARTICLE 1. . . . And pursuant to an act of Congress approved May 28, 1830, the United States do hereby forever secure and guarantee the lands embraced within the said limits, to the members of the Choctaw and Chickasaw tribes, their heirs and successors, to be held in common; so that each and every member of either tribe shall have an equal, undivided interest in the whole: Provided, however, No part thereof shall ever be sold without the

consent of both tribes, and that said land shall revert to the United States if said Indians and their heirs become extinct or abandon the same.

ARTICLE 5. The members of either the Choctaw or the Chickasaw tribe, shall have the right, freely, to settle within the jurisdiction of the other, and shall thereupon be entitled to all the rights, privileges, and immunities of citizens thereof; but no member of either tribe shall be entitled to participate in the funds belonging to the other tribe. Citizens of both tribes shall have the right to institute and prosecute suits in the courts of either, under such regulations as may, from time to time, be prescribed by their respective legislatures.

ARTICLE 6. Any person duly charged with a criminal offence against the laws of either the Choctaw or the Chickasaw tribe, and escaping into the jurisdiction of the other, shall be promptly surrendered, upon the demand of the proper authorities of the tribe, within whose jurisdiction the offence shah be alleged to have been committed.

ARTICLE 7. So far as may be compatible with the Constitution of the United States and the laws made in pursuance thereof, regulating trade and intercourse with the Indian tribes, the Choctaws and Chickasaws shall be secured in the unrestricted right of self-government, and full jurisdiction, over persons and property, within their respective limits; excepting, however, all persons, with their property, who are not by birth, adoption, or otherwise citizens or members of either the Choctaw or Chickasaw tribe, and all persons not being citizens or members of either tribe, found within their limits, shall be considered intruders, and be removed from, and kept out of the same, by the United States agent, assisted if necessary by the military, with the following exceptions, viz: Such individuals as are now, or may be in the employment of the Government, and their families; those peacefully travelling, or temporarily sojourning in the country or trading therein, under license from the proper authority of the United States, and such as may be permitted by the Choctaws or Chickasaws, with the assent of the United States agent, to reside within their limits, without becoming citizens or members of either of said tribes.

15. J R

TREATY WITH THE CREEKS, ETC. {1856, Aug. 7} 11 Stat., 699. Ratified Aug. 16, 1856. Proclaimed Aug. 28, 1856.

ARTICLE 14. Any person duly charged with a criminal offense

Appendix D 127

against the laws of either the Creek or Seminole tribe, and escaping into the jurisdiction of the other, shall be promptly surrendered upon the demand of the proper authority of the tribe within whose jurisdiction the offense shall be alleged to have been committed.

ARTICLE 15. So far as may be compatible with the Constitution of the United States, and the laws made in pursuance thereof, regulating trade and intercourse with the Indian tribes, the Creeks and Seminoles shall be secured in the unrestricted right of self-government, and full jurisdiction over persons and property, within their respective limits; excepting, however, all white persons, with their property, who are not, by adoption or otherwise, members of either the Creek or Seminole tribe; and all persons not being members of either tribe, found within their limits, shall be considered intruders, and be removed from and kept out of the same by the United States agents for said tribes, respectively; (assisted, if necessary, by the military ;) with the following exceptions, viz: such individuals with their families as may be in the employment of the Government of the United States; all persons peaceably travelling, or temporarily sojourning in the country, or trading therein under license from the proper authority of the United States; and such persons as may be permitted by the Creeks or Seminoles, with the assent of the proper authorities of the United States, to reside within their respective limits without becoming members of either of said tribes.

16. L G R
TREATY WITH THE SEMINOLE {1866, Mar. 21} 14 Stat., 755. Ratified, July 19, 1866. Proclaimed, Aug. 16, 1866.

ARTICLE 7. The Seminole Nation agrees to such legislation as Congress and the President may deem necessary for the better administration of the rights of person and property within the Indian Territory: Provided, however, (that) said legislation shall not in any manner interfere with or annul their present tribal organization, rights, laws, privileges, and customs.

17. C L G R
TREATY WITH THE CHOCTAW AND CHICKASAW {1866, Apr. 28} 14 Stat., 769. Ratified June 28, 1866. Proclaimed July 10, 1866.

ARTICLE 4. The said nations further agree that all negroes, not otherwise disqualified or disabled, shall be competent witnesses in all civil and criminal suits and proceedings in the Choctaw and Chickasaw courts, any law to the contrary notwithstanding . . .

ARTICLE 7. The Choctaws and Chickasaws agree to such legislation as Congress and the President of the United States may deem necessary for the better administration of justice and the protection of the rights of person and property within the Indian Territory: Provided, however, Such legislation shall not in anywise interfere with or annul their present tribal organization, or their respective legislatures or judiciaries, or the rights, laws, privileges, or customs of the Choctaw and Chickasaw Nations respectively.

Eighth. The Choctaws and Chickasaws also agree that a court or courts may be established in said Territory with such jurisdiction and organization as Congress may prescribe: Provided, That the same shall not interfere with the local judiciary of either of said nations

18. J L G R
TREATY WITH THE CREEKS {1866, June 14} Ratified July 1866. Proclaimed Aug. 11. 1866
ARTICLE 2. The Creeks hereby covenant and agree that henceforth neither slavery nor involuntary servitude, otherwise than in the punishment of crimes, whereof the parties shall have been duly convicted in accordance with laws applicable to all members of said tribe, shall ever exist in said nation; and inasmuch as there are among the Creeks many persons of African descent, who have no interest in the soil, it is stipulated that hereafter these persons lawfully residing in said Creek country under their laws and usages, or who have been thus residing in said country, and may return within one year from the ratification of this treaty, and their descendants and such others of the same race as may be permitted by the laws of the said nation to settle within the limits of the jurisdiction of the Creek Nation as citizens (thereof,) shall have and enjoy all the rights and privileges of native citizens, including an equal interest in the soil and national funds, and the laws of the said nation shall be equally binding upon and give equal protection to all such persons, and all others, of whatsoever race or color, who may be adopted as citizens or members of said tribe.

ARTICLE 3. In compliance with the desire of the United States to locate other Indians and freedmen thereon, the Creeks hereby cede and convey to the United States, to be sold to and used as homes for such other civilized Indians as the United States may choose to

Appendix D 129

settle thereon, the west half of their entire domain, to be divided by a line running north and south; the eastern half of said Creek lands, being retained by them, shall, except as herein otherwise stipulated, be forever set apart as a home for said Creek Nation . . .
ARTICLE 10. The Creeks agree to such legislation as Congress and the President of the United States may deem necessary for the better administration of justice and the protection of the rights of person and property within the Indian territory: Provided, however, (That) said legislation shall not in any manner interfere with or annul their present tribal organization, rights, laws, privileges, and customs. The Creeks also agree that a general council, consisting of delegates elected by each nation or tribe lawfully resident within the Indian territory, may be annually convened in said territory, which council shall be organized in such manner and possess such powers as are hereinafter described.

19. J C G
TREATY WITH THE CHEROKEE {1866, July 19} 14 Stat., 799. Ratified July 27, 1866. Proclaimed Aug. 11, 1866.
ARTICLE 2. Amnesty is hereby declared by the United States and the Cherokee Nation for all crimes and misdemeanors committed by one Cherokee on the person or property of another Cherokee, or of a citizen of the United States, prior to the fourth day of July, eighteen hundred and sixty-six; and no right of action arising out of wrongs committed in aid or in the suppression of the rebellion shall be prosecuted or maintained in the courts of the United States or in the courts of the Cherokee Nation.
ARTICLE 13. The Cherokees also agree that a court or courts may be established by the United States in said Territory, with such jurisdiction and organized in such manner as may be prescribed by law: Provided. That the judicial tribunals of the nation shall be allowed to retain exclusive jurisdiction in all civil and criminal cases arising within their country in which members of the nation, by nativity or adoption, shall be the only parties, or where the cause of action shall arise in the Cherokee Nation, except as otherwise provided in this treaty.
ARTICLE 14. The right to the use and occupancy of a quantity of land not exceeding one hundred and sixty acres, to be selected according to legal subdivisions in one body, and to include their improvements, and not including the improvements of any member of the Cherokee Nation, is hereby granted to every society or denomination which has erected, or which with the consent of the

national council may hereafter erect, buildings within the Cherokee country for missionary or educational purposes. But no land thus granted, nor buildings which have been or may be erected thereon, shall ever be sold or (o)therwise disposed of except with the consent and approval of the Cherokee national council and the Secretary of the Interior. And whenever any such-lands or buildings shall be sold or disposed of, the proceeds thereof shall be applied by said society or societies for like purposes within said nation, subject to the approval of the Secretary of the Interior.

20. J
TREATY WITH THE POTAWATOMI {1867, Feb. 27} 15 Stat., 531. Ratified July 25, 1868. Proclaimed, Aug. 7, 1868.
ARTICLE 3. After such reservation shall have been selected and set apart for the Pottawatomies, it shall never be included within the jurisdiction of any State or Territory, unless an Indian Territory shall be organized, as provided for in certain treaties made in eighteen hundred and Sixty-six with the Choctaws and other tribes occupying "Indian country;" in which case, or in case of the organization of a legislative council or other body, for the regulation of matters affecting the relations of the tribes to each other, the Pottawatomies resident thereon shall have the right to representation, according to their numbers, on equal terms with the other tribes.

Works Cited

Abel, Annie Heloise. *The American Indian as Slaveholder and Secessionist*. Cleveland: Arthur H. Clark, 1915; reprint, Lincoln and London: University of Nebraska, 1992.

Andrist, Ralph K. *The Long Death: The Last Days of the Plains Indian*. New York: Collier Books, 1969; New Collier Books, 1993.

Baker, Ray Stannard and William E. Dodd, editors. *The Public Papers of Woodrow Wilson*, Volume II. New York: Harper, 1926.

Berkhofer, Robert F., Jr. *The White Man's Indian*. New York: Vintage Books, 1979.

Black, Henry Campbell. *Black's Law Dictionary*. 6th Edition by the publishers editorial staff, Joseph R. Nolan, Jacqueline M. Nolan-Haley, M.J. Connolly, Stephen C. Hicks, and Martina N. Alibrandi. St. Paul: West Publishing, 1990.

Brophie, William and Sophie Aberle. *The Indian: America's Unfinished Business*. Norman, University of Oklahoma, 1966.

Caster, David and Oscar Parsons. "Locus of Control in Alcoholics and Treatment Outcomes," *Journal of Studies on Alcohol*. New Brunswick: Rutgers Center of Alcohol Studies. 38:11 (1977).

The Center for the Study of Indian Law and Policy, the University of Oklahoma and The Center for Tribal Studies, Northeastern State University, Tahlequah. *Trying a New Way: The Independent Assessment Report on the Self-Governance Demonstration Project*. Washington, D.C.: Government Printing Office, 1991.

Claiborne, Louis F. "The Trend of Supreme Court Decisions in Indian Cases" *American Indian Law Review*, 22 (1999).

Clark, Blue. *Lone Wolf v. Hitchcock: Treaty Rights and Indian Law at the End of the Nineteenth Century.* Law in the American West Volume. 5. Lincoln and London: University of Nebraska, 1994.

_____. (Carter Blue Clark). "The New Deal for Indians," *Between Two Worlds.* edited by Arell Morgan Gibson. The Oklahoma Series Volume 22. Oklahoma Historical Society, 1986.

Cohen, Felix S. *Handbook of Federal Indian Law*. Washington D.C.: Bureau of Printing, 1943; reprint, Buffalo: William S. Hein, 1988.

Debo, Angie. *And Still the Waters Run: The Betrayal of the Five Civilized Tribes.* Princeton: Princeton University, 1940; reprint Norman and London: University of Oklahoma, 1989.

_____. *A History of the Indians of the United States,* The Civilization of the American Indian Series Volume 106. Norman and London: University of Oklahoma, 1970.

_____. *The Rise and Fall of the Choctaw Republic.* The Civilization of the American Indian Series Volume 6. Norman and London: University of Oklahoma, 1961.

Deloria, Vine, Jr. *Custer Died for Your Sins.* Norman and London: University of Oklahoma Press, 1988.

Deloria, Vine, Jr. and Clifford Lytle. *American Indians American Justice.* .Austin: University of Texas, 1983.

de Tocqueville, Alexis. *Democracy in America.* Edited by J. P. Maayer, translated by George Lawrence. New York: Harper and Row, 1966; HarperCollins 19th edition.

Farmer, Richard N. *Benevolent Aggression: The Necessary Impact of the Advanced Nations on Indigenous Peoples.* .New York: David McKay, 1972.

Fehrenbach, T.R., *Comanches: The Destruction of a People* .New York: Alfred A. Knopf, 1974; New York: Da Capo, 1994.

Fenna, D., *et al.* "Ethanol Metabolism in Various Racial Groups", *Canadian Medical Association Journal* 105 (1971).

Forrest, Gary G. *Alcoholism and Human Sexuality.* Springfield: Charles C. Thomas Publisher, 1983.

Gage, N. L. and David C. Berliner. *Educational Psychology.* Chicago: Rand McNally College Publishing Company, 1975.

Fixico, Donald L. "Termination and Relocation: Federal Indian Policy in the 1950's." Ph.D. dissertation. University of Oklahoma, 1980.

Galbraith, John Kenneth. *The Nature of Mass Poverty.* Cambridge and London: Harvard University, 1979.

Gallaher, Margaret M., *et al.* "Pedestrian and Hypothermia Deaths Among Native Americans in New Mexico". *Journal of the American Medical Association* 267:10 (1992).

Works Cited

Getches, David H., Charles F. Wilkinson and Robert A. Williams, Jr. *Federal Indian Law: Cases and Materials*, 3rd edition. St. Paul: West Publishing, 1993.

Goldberg, Carole E. "Public Law 280: The limits of State Jurisdiction Over Reservation Indians." *U.C.L.A. Law Review,* 22 (1975).

Hays, J. E., editor. *Indian Treaties: Cessions of Land in Georgia 1705–1837*, .W.P.A. Project No. 7158, 1941.

Hoig, Stan. *The Sand Creek Massacre.* Norman: University of Oklahoma, 1961.

Hoxie, Frederick E. *A Final Promise: The Campaign to Assimilate the Indians, 1880–1920.* Lincoln and London: University of Nebraska, 1984.

Jones-Saumty, Deborah, Larry Hochhaus, Ralph Dru and Arthur Zeiner. "Psychological Factors of Familial Alcoholism in American Indians and Caucasians," *Journal of Clinical Psychology.* Brandon VT: Clinical Psychology Publishing Company, 39:5 (1983).

Kappler, Charles J. *Indian Treaties 1778–1883.* Mattituck New York: Amereon House, 1972; reprint of *Indian Affairs: Treaties and Laws,* Volume II, Treaties, Washington D.C.: GPO, 1904.

Kehrer, Kenneth. "Education, Race and Poverty," in *Perspectives on Poverty.* Dennis J. Dugan and William H. Leahy, editors. .New York: Praeger, 1973.

Korman, Sharon. *The Right of Conquest: The Acquisition of Territory by Force in International Law and Practice.* Oxford: Clarendon Press, 1996.

Lewis, Oscar. "The Culture of Poverty," *Scientific American* 215 (1966).

Lipton, Michael. *Why People Stay Poor: Urban Bias in World Development.* Cambridge: Harvard University, 1977.

Locke, John. *Two Treatises of Government.* Peter Laslett, editor. Cambridge Texts in the History of Political Thought Series. Cambridge and New York: Cambridge University, 1988.

Lujan, Carol Chiago. "Alcohol-related Deaths of American Indians, Stereotypes and Strategies," *Journal of the American Medical Association* 267:10 (1992).

May, Phillip A. "The Epidemiology of Alcohol Abuse," *American Indian Culture and Research Journal* 18: 2 (1994).

McLuhan, T.C. *Touch the Earth: A Self-portrait of Indian Existence.* New York: Promontory Press, 1971.

Merriam, C.E. *History of the Theory of Sovereignty Since Rousseau.* Studies in History, Economics and Public Law Volume XII, Number 4. New York: Columbia University, 1900.

Miller, S. M. "The Great Chain of Poverty Explanations," *Poverty: A*

Global Review. Else Oyen, S. M. Miller and Syed Abdus Samad, editors. Oslo and Paris: Scandinavian University Press and UNESCO, 1996.

Mouly, George J., *Psychology for Effective Teaching,* 2nd Edition. London and New York: Holt Rinehart and Winston Inc., 1968.

Nabokov, Peter, *Native American Testimony: A Chronicle of Indian-White Relations from Prophecy to the Present, 1492–1992,* New York: Penguin, 1991.

Nerburn, Kent and Mengelkoch, Louise, editors. *Native American Wisdom.* The Classic Wisdom Collection..San Rafael CA: New World Library, 1991.

Parker, Linda S. "The Indian Citizenship Act of 1924," *Between Two Worlds: The Survival of Twentieth Century Indians.* Edited by Arrell Morgan Gibson. The Oklahoma Series Volume 22. Oklahoma Historical Society, 1986.

Pickles, Tim. *New Orleans 1815: Andrew Jackson Crushes the British.* Osprey Military Campaign Series Volume 28, edited by David G. Chandler. London: Osprey, 1993.

Prucha, Francis Paul. *American Indian Policy in the Formative Years: The Trade and Intercourse Acts, 1790–1834.* Cambridge: Harvard University, 1962.

_____. ed., *Documents of United States Indian Policy ,* 2nd Expanded Edition. Lincoln and London: University of Nebraska, 1990.

_____. *The Great Father.* Bison Books paperback combined and unabridged volumes 1 and 2 edition, 1995; Lincoln and London: University of Nebraska, 1984.

Reed, Warren, editor. *Public Papers of the Presidents of the United States: Lyndon B. Johnson, 1968–69.* Washington D.C.: Government Printing Office, 1970.

Rescher, Nicholas. "American Philosophy," *The Oxford Companion to Philosophy,* Ted Honderich, editor. New York: Oxford University Press, 1995.

Reyhner, Jon, editor. *Teaching American Indian Students.* Norman and London: University of Oklahoma Press, 1992.

Richardson, James, editor. *Messages and Papers of the Presidents.* Washington: Bureau of National Literature, 1911.

Rosenman, Samuel, editor. *Public Papers and Addresses of Franklin D. Roosevelt, 1934.* New York: Random House, 1938.

Samad, Syed Abdus. "The Present Situation in Poverty Research," *Poverty: A Global Review.* Edited by Else Oyen, S. M. Miller and Syed Abdus Samad. Oslo and Paris: Scandinavian University Press and UNESCO, 1996.

Sarbin, Theodore R. "The Culture of Poverty, Social Identity and Cognitive Outcomes," *Psychological Factors in Poverty*. Edited by Vernon L. Allen. Chicago: Markham,1970.

Stanfield, Rochelle. "Getting Out the Tribal Vote," *National Journal*. Washington D.C.: National Journal Inc., 1992.

Stratton, Ray, Arthur Zeiner and Alfonso Paredes. "Tribal Affiliation and Prevalence of Alcohol Problems," *Journal of Studies on Alcohol*. New Brunswick: Publication Division of the Rutgers Center of Alcohol Studies. 39:7 (1978).

Strickland, Rennard, "Genocide-At-Law: An Historical and Contemporary View of the Native American Experience," *University of Kansas Law Review* 34.

Swinson, Richard and Derek Eaves. *Alcoholism and Addiction*. London: Woburn Press, 1978.,

Sword, Wiley. *President Washington's Indian War: The Struggle for the Old Northwest 1790–1795*. Norman and London: University of Oklahoma, 1985.

Thomas, George. *Poverty in the Non-Metropolitan South: A Causal Explanation*. Lexington Massachusetts: Lexington Books, 1972.

Thornton, Russell. *American Indian Holocaust and Survival: A Population History Since 1492*. Norman and London: University of Oklahoma, 1987.

U.S. Bureau of the Census. *Statistical Abstract of the United States 1995*. Washington, D.C.: U.S. Government Printing Office.

U.S. Indian Health Service. *Regional Differences in Indian Health*. Washington D.C.: Department of Health and Human Services, Division of Program Statistics, 1994.

U.S. Indian Health Service. *Trends In Indian Health—1994*. Washington D.C.: Department of Health and Human Services, 1994.

U.S. Office of Indian Affairs *Indians in the War*, .Lawrence Kansas: Haskell Printing Department, 1945.

Utley, Robert M. and Wolcombe E. Washburn. *Indian Wars*. Boston: Houghton Mifflin, 1977.

Vanderwerth, W.C., *Indian Oratory: Famous Speeches By Noted Chieftains*, The Civilization of the American Indian Series, volume 110, Norman and London: University of Oklahoma, 1971.

Webster, Daniel. *The Works of Daniel Webster*, Volume III. Boston: Charles C. Little and James Brown, 1851.

White, Richard. *The Roots of Dependency: Subsistence, Environment and Social Change Among the Choctaws, Pawnees, and Navajos*. Lincoln and London: University of Nebraska, 1983.

Wilkins, David E. *American Indian Sovereignty and the U.S. Supreme*

Court: The Masking of Justice. Austin: University of Texas, 1997.

Wilkinson, Charles F. *American Indians, Time, and the Law: Native Societies in a Modern Constitutional Democracy.* New Haven and London: Yale, 1987.

Williams Jr., Robert A. *The American Indian in Western Legal Thought.* New York and Oxford: Oxford University, 1990.

_____. *Linking Arms Together: American Indian Treaty Visions of Law and Peace, 1600–1800.* New York and London: Routledge, 1999.

Wilson, James, *The Earth Shall Weep: A History of Native America*, New York: Grove, 1998.

Witkins, Alexandra "To Silence a Drum: The Imposition of United States Citizenship on Native Peoples," *Historical Reflections/Réflexions Historiques.* New York: Alfred University. 21:2 (1995).

Woolfolk, Anita E. *Educational Psychology,* 4th Edition. New Jersey: Prentice Hall, 1990.

Wright, Esmond. "Fabric of Freedom 1763–1800," *The Making of America.* David Donald, editor. London: Macmillan, 1965.

Wunder, John R., *Retained by the People: A History of American Indians and the Bill of Rights,* New York and Oxford: Oxford University, 1994.

Zeiner, Arthur. "Psychological Factors of Familial Alcoholism in American Indians and Caucasians," *Journal of Clinical Psychology.* Brandon VT: Clinical Psychology Publishing Company. 39:5 (1983).

Cases Cited

Blatchford v. Native Village of Noatak, 501 U.S. 775 (1991).
Cherokee Nation v. Georgia, 5 Peters 1 (1831).
Elk v. Wilkins, 112 U.S. 94 (1884).
Johnson v. McIntosh, 8 Wheaton 543 (1823).
Lone Wolf v. Hitchcock, 187 U.S. 553 (1903).
Mackey v. Coxe, 18 How. 100 (1855).
M'Culloch v. State of Maryland, 17 U.S. 316 (1819).
Merrion v. Jicarilla Apache Tribe, 455 U.S. 130 (1982).
Principality of Monaco v. State of Mississippi, 219 U.S. 313 (1934).
United States v. Kagama, 118 U.S. 375 (1886).
United States v. Joseph, 94 U.S. 614 (1876).
United States v. Sandoval, 231 U.S. 28 (1913).
United States v. Tobacco, 28 Fed. Cas., 195 (1870).
United States v. Wheeler, 435 U.S. 313 (1978).
United States v. Wong Kim Ark, 169 U.S. 649 (1898).
Worcester v. Georgia, 6 Peters 515 (1832).

Index

Adams, John Quincy, 36, 41
Alabama, 38
Alcoholism *see* Health
Allotment, 67–8, 70–7
    Allotment Prior to Dawes Act, 69–70
    Justifications for, 67–9
    and Land Tenure, 107
    Loss of Land as a Result, 74–5
    Outcome of, 74–5
    Swindles, 74
Arapahoe, 55–6
Assimilation, 20, 56, 65, 80, 82
Bison *see* Buffalo
Black Kettle 55
Blatchford v. Native Village of Noatak, 96, 98
Board of Indian Commissioners, 67–8
Boarding Schools *see* Schools, BIA
Buchanan, James, 54
Buffalo, 60–1
van Buren, Martin, 50, 101
California, 53
Caldwell, District Judge, 62
Cherokee, 6, 20, 39, 43, 44–50, 54–5
Cherokee Nation v. Georgia, 44–46
Cheyenne, 55–6

Chickasaw, 20, 39, 55
Chivington, John, 55
Choctaw, 6, 20, 37, 39, 43, 53, 54, 55, 71
Citizenship, Indian, 71, 76–7, 98, 111
Citizenship Act, 76–7
Civilization Fund Act, 25
Civil Rights Act, 82–4
Civil War, U.S., 54, 56
Civil War, Indian Nation, 54
Cleveland, Grover, 69–71
Commerce Clause, 62, 98–9
Confederacy, 54
Conquest, 33–4, 39, 42, 101–102
Corruption, U.S.
    as Cause of Indian Unrest 57
Creek, 20, 39, 53
Crow, Dog, 62–3
Curtis Act, 72
Custer, George Armstrong, 58
Dawes Act *see* Allotment
Dawes Commission, 72
Dawes, Henry, 67
Doctrine of Discovery, 32, 34, 64, 103–6 and *see also Johnson v. McIntosh, Terra Nullius, Mabo V. Queensland*

139

Dodge, Richard I., 60
Economics, 5–6, 7–11, 92
Education, 6, 11–2, 92
Eisenhower, Dwight, 82
Enabling Act, 73
Evans, John, 55
ex Parte Crow Dog, 62–3
Five Tribes, 20, 71, 72–5
Five Civilized Tribes *see* Five Tribes
Foreign Nation, Indian Nations as, 38, 44–6
General Allotment Act *see* Allotment
George III, King of England, 21
Georgia, 23, 27, 34, 36–9, 40, 41, 43, 46–7, 50
Georgia Compact, 34, 36, 40
Government, Indian Nation, 35–36, 38–39,
Grant, Ulysses, 56–58
Guardianship, 45–46, 49, 56–7, 62, 64, 75, 78–79, 92, 99, 102
Health, 6–7, 12–14, 92
Income *see* Economics
Indian Citizenship Act *see* Citizenship Act
Indian Civil Rights Act *see* Civil Rights Act
Indian Removal Act *see* Removal Act
Indian Reorganization Act, 78–80
Indian Territory, 50–1
Intruders/Intrusion *see* Settler Imperialism
Jackson, Andrew, 34–9, 41, 43, 46, 50, 100
Jefferson, Thomas, 20, 23–4, 26, 39
Johnson, Lyndon, 82–3
Johnson O'Malley Act, 6
Johnson v. McIntosh, 32–4, 36, 40–3, 49, 99–103, 104, 105, 107, 110
Jurisdiction
    Federal, 63–64
    State, 36, 38, 63–4, 100 and *see also* Public Law-280
Kansas, 51
Kansas Nebraska Act, 51
Kiowa, 75–6
Land *see* Title
Leup, Francis, 72
Locus of Control (LOC), 14–5, 92, 93 and *see also* Motivation
Lone Wolf v. Hitchcock, 75
Louisiana Purchase, 26–27
Mabo v. Queensland, 108–109
Mackey v. Cox, 62, 98
Major Crimes Act, 63
Marshall, John, 46–9, 98, 99–103, 110
Marshall, Thurgood, 97
McLean, John, 49–50, 62, 100, 103
Menominee, 81
Meriam Report, 78
Miller, Samuel, 63–5
Monroe, James, 34–6
Motivation, 11–12 and *see also* Locus of Control
Navajo, 6
Nebraska, 51, 82
North Carolina, 22
Ownership *see* Title
Oklahoma, 51, 73
Oklahoma Organic Act, 71
Omaha, 82
Osage, 55
Parker, Ely S., 61
Peace Policy, 56–8, 61
Plenary Power, 75, 92, 94, 96, 98–99, 103, 104, 107, 110–3
Popular Sovereignty *see* Sovereignty, Popular
Poverty *see* Economics
Proclamation Line of 1763, 21
Property *see* Title
Public Law-280, 81–2
Principality of Monaco v. State of Mississippi, 96

Index

Pueblo, 59
Quapaw, 55
Religion, 105
Removal, 28, 31–2, 36, 53, 101
Removal Act, 40, 42, 50
Roosevelt, Franklin, 78
Roosevelt, Theodore, 73
Sand Creek Massacre, 55–6
Schools, BIA, 77–78
Self-Determination, 82, 84, 101–102
   and *see also* Self-Governance
Self Determination and Education Assistance Act, 84, 93
Self-Governance, 1, 19–20, 26, 43, 48, 50, 53–54, 78–79, 83, 84–86, 93–4
Self-Governance Act, 84–6
Seminole, 20, 53
Seneca, 55
Settler Imperialism, 20–22, 34, 50–51
   as Cause of Indian Unrest, 23–24
   against Cherokee, 22–3, 36
   Explanation of , 20–1
   Incidents of, 22–3
   Reasons for, 20–1, 25–6
   Tocqueville's account of, 42–3
Shawnee, 55
Sheridan, Phillip Henry, 58, 61
Sherman, William Tecumseh, 58, 61
Sioux, 56
   Brûlé, 62
   Santee, 55
Society of Friends, 56–7
Sovereign Immunity, 86, 96–7
Sovereignty (Indian)
   Abolition of Indian Governments, 72
   Inherent, 1, 86, 98–9, 110–1, 113
   Retained, 1, 101, 110
   Indian Attempts to Protect, 33, 43, 54, 75, 85, 101–2
   U.S. Diminution of, 64, 91–3, 100, 103
   U.S. Recognition of, 20, 22, 35, 36, 43, 84–6 and *see also* Self-Governance
Sovereignty, Divided, 94, 96
Sovereignty, Popular, 94, 97, 101–2, 104, 110–3
Spotted Tail, 62–63
Terra Nullius, 108–9
Termination Act, 80–81
Title
   Fee-simple, 43
   Indian, 33, 40, 63–4, 99–100, 103–4
   Locke and, 105–7
   of Occupancy *see* Title, Indian
de Tocqueville, Alexis, 42–3
Trade and Intercourse Acts, 24–5, 41–3
Trail of Tears, 53, and *see also* Removal
Treaty (ies), 20, 22 and Appendix D
   Cherokee, 48
   of 1763, 21
   End of Treatymaking, 61
   Failure of U.S. to enforce, 24, 27, 31–2 and *see also* Settler Imperialism
   of Hopewell, 22
   of 1820, 43
   Indian View of, 27
   of Medicine Lodge, 75
   Repudiation by U.S., 31–2, 75, 76, 86
United States v. Joseph, 59
United States v. Kagama, 62–64, 99, 104–5
United States v. Lucero, 59
United States v. Tobacco, 62
United States v. Wheeler, 92
Wards, Indians as *see* Guardianship
Washington, George, 22–4, 25

Webster, Daniel, 94
White, Edward, 75–76
Wheeler-Howard Act *see* Indian
  Reorganization Act
Wilson, Woodrow, 101–102
Winnebago, 82
Worcester v. Georgia, 46–7, 62, 103–4
Worcester, Samuel, 46–7, 50
World War II, 77–8, 80

ISBN 978-1-138-97884-3

an *informa* business

www.routledge.com